Rental Property Investing

How to Build a Passive Income Business: the Keys to Manage and Achieve Success with Short and Long Term Investment

Gabriele Undig

Table of Contents

Introduction
Chapter 1: Real Estate Investing
    What Real Estate Investing Entails
    Why You Should Choose Real Estate Investment
    What Makes Real Estate a Good Investment
    Benefits of Investing in Real Estate

Chapter 2: How to Build Passive Income Through Real Estate
    The Keys to Manage and Achieve Success with Short-Term and Long-Term Investment

Chapter 3: Real Estate Networking and Its Importance
    Importance of Networking in Real Estate
    Tips for Networking in Real Estate

Chapter 4: The Best Ways to Finance Your Real Estate Deals
    Financial Freedom Blueprint
    Steps to Achieve Financial Independence
    Effective Ways to Finance Your Real Estate Deal
    Guidelines for Funding Your First Real Estate

Chapter 5: Evaluating, Managing, and Adding Value to Property
    Evaluating Property
        Steps to Evaluate a Property Investment
    Managing Property

    Adding Value to Property

    How to Give Back To the Market

Chapter 6: The Best Rental Investing Strategies

    What to Expect in the Rental Investment

    Strategies to Use in the Rental Investment Sector

        BRRR Strategy

        Fix and Flip

        Long-Term and Short-Term Rentals

        Commercial Real Estate Strategy

        Marketing Your Rental Property

Chapter 7: Detailed Information About Real Estate Investing

    Types of Real Estate

    An Outline of the Real Estate Business Industry

    Why People Enter into Real Estate Business

    Appreciation in Real Estate

    How to Earn Income in Real Estate

    Terms Used in Real Estate Business

    More Benefits of Real Estate Business

Chapter 8: Tips on Assembling an Incredible Real Estate Team

    Pros of a Real Estate Team

    Professionals Required in the Real Estate Team

    Tips for Putting Together the Best Real Estate Team

Chapter 9: Real Estate Exit Strategy

    Importance of Real Estate Exit Strategies

Choosing the Right Real Estate Strategy

Real Estate Exit Strategies

Chapter 10: The Four Secrets of the Successful Apartment Building Investor

Ways of Finding Best Deals

Conclusion

Introduction

Congratulations on purchasing *Real Estate Investing,* and thank you for doing so. The world is growing, and many people, especially families, are looking for homes to establish and grow. Investors have therefore ventured into putting their money in real estate business with the number rising each passing day. Becoming successful in the sector is henceforth mandatory despite the competition out there. This book is, therefore, the first step to learning different techniques to stand out from the rest.

The following chapters will discuss the primary aspects of how to succeed in real estate business as well as the secrets to build your reputation. Investing in anything is usually risky, mainly when you have limited knowledge about your field of the venture. In most cases, some learn the general idea about the topic but fail to understand the details of how to prosper. This means you will want to contemplate all the essential elements of the industry before investing in it. You will then learn different secrets used by investors to make complete their deals without the chances of investing in unsuccessful businesses.

That said, the secrets will consist of different forms of how to successfully go about in deals without any issues. You will learn about how to raise money essential for your first deal and to get your offer approved without any complications. Besides, another secret will entail how to learn deal analysis and complete sales within a shorter time. Despite the existence of many deals out there, you will learn how to find ways of accessing the best deals in the market.

There are plenty of books on this subject on the market, so thanks again for choosing this one! Every effort was made to ensure it is full of as much useful information as possible. Please enjoy!

Chapter 1: Real Estate Investing

Careful considerations are required before making any investment decision. You have to first weigh the risks involved in a particular investment, and then look at the returns. The research process could be daunting. Unfortunately, you can still get the investment wrong and lose your money.

On your quest to invest in real estate, due diligence is of the essence, but you will realize that there are not many loopholes as you would encounter with other types of investment.

In this book, we are going to demystify real estate investing. At the end of it, you should have a clear idea as to why you should choose real estate investing and all the benefits that come with investing in it.

With that being said, choosing real estate investing could be one of the best investment decisions you can ever make.

What Real Estate Investing Entails

Real estate investing revolves around purchasing, owning, selling, or renting out a property to make a profit. It might be capital-intensive, but it remains to be one of the safest types of investment.

An understanding of property markets is a prerequisite in real estate investment. As much as there are many property management firms to work with, you will still need to learn the ropes of the investment. Once you understand the dynamics of the trade, there is no reason why you should not be successful.

Why You Should Choose Real Estate Investment

There are numerous reasons you should invest your money in real estate. Before we delve into that, let us have a look at what makes a good investment. Here are some characteristics of a good investment:

Safety. Every shrewd businessperson is interested in knowing the risks involved in a particular investment. The right decision is always to invest your money in something that's not volatile. Otherwise, you will end up losing all your money.

Therefore, a good investment has to be safe. The more money you invest, the harder the losses are likely to hit you. That is why you should always invest your money wisely.

Predictable Outcome. A great investment should have a predictable outcome. You ought to know what your chances of making a profit look like. Since investments are not just about profits, you also need to know the kind of losses you can make, just in case your investment does not work out.

Demand. Demand dictates profits in every investment. When you invest in something not in demand, chances are that you are going to dispose of it at a loss. On the other hand, it is likely to make you money. Besides that, where buying and selling is concerned, it is prudent to put your money in an asset that can sell fast.

Consistent Payouts. A good investment pays consistently. This could be in the short-term or long-term. If you are going to invest in a long-term endeavor, the returns should be convincing. For short-term investment, the returns should be reasonable.

Easy to Sell or Buy. Most investments are all about buying and selling. You buy an asset today, wait for it to appreciate, and sell it at a profit in after some time. If an investment allows you to do so, then it is a good investment.

If you closely examine real estate investing, you will realize that it is a good investment as it meets all the conditions listed above, but know that this does not happen automatically.

You ought to conduct thorough research before buying a property. As much as real estate investing is promising, it demands research and sound decision-making. Therefore, you should take the time to study the location as well as the real estate market in a given area.

What Makes Real Estate a Good Investment

Real estate is a fantastic investment when done right. It is an excellent investment, both as long-term and short-term. Here are some of the reasons why real estate investing is a wonderful choice.

Active and passive income. Many investments will not give you both an active and passive income, but real estate can. For example, if you acquire an apartment, you can rent it out at a reasonable rate. You will make a passive income regularly until you decide to sell the apartment.

After a few years, the apartment is likely to have appreciated. Should you opt to sell it, you will make a one-off profit, which qualifies as an active income. This makes real estate investing lucrative.

Stable income. If you desire an income that is not subject to negative fluctuations, real estate is the way to go. Buying a complex and then renting it out undoubtedly provides a stable income.

A real estate investment is not as volatile as stocks or other types of investments. Renting out a property gives you a regular and reliable income. This is the kind of income that you probably can't easily get elsewhere.

Safe investment. Every investment comes with a risk. A shrewd investor should always settle for a low-risk investment but targets high returns. Real estate is a low-risk investment. You can invest in it diligently and mitigate the risks.

This is dependent on your expertise. If you are not an expert, you could always consult. From a buying and selling perspective, real estate is quite safe. When you buy a piece of land or property, you will barely sell it as a loss.

If the property depreciates, all is not lost. In most cases, you should be able to recoup most of your investment through selling. You can also invest in a way that ensures you do not lose more than the equity invested.

Depreciation. Most assets are subject to depreciation. For example, if you buy a vehicle today, you will sell it for less than you bought in just a few months. The best thing about buying a property is that it appreciates over time.

Instead of becoming worthless, real estate goes up in value. When you decide to sell it, you are guaranteed to make a profit.

Physical asset. A physical asset is more comforting than money tied down in stocks. You know where your property is located and that it will not just disappear into thin air. You certainly will not lose your sleep over this type of investment.

Real estate allows you to add value. One of the ways to profit in real estate is to add value to a property and then sell it. You can buy an old duplex and upgrade it by installing modern facilities, or you can remodel it and sell it at a higher price. This is not something you can easily pull off with other investments.

Benefits of Investing in Real Estate

Long-term financial security. Everybody thinks of securing their financial future. We worry ourselves wondering what is going to happen after retirement. Once the paycheck stops coming, you will still need money to take care of yourself and your children. The good news is that investing in real estate can help you secure your financial future.

When you invest in rental property, you start earning a steady income. Such an income is reliable; it is long-lasting and could help you secure your financial future for a lifetime.

Tax benefits. Most streams of income are subject to heavy taxation. If you are employed, a certain percentage of your salary is deducted by the government. The same case applies when you are running a business.

Real estate comes with numerous tax benefits. As a rental property owner, you are exempted from the self-employment tax. The government is also generous in offering tax breaks for property maintenance, depreciation, property taxes, and insurance. Additionally, there are lower tax rates for long-term real estate investments.

Real estate appreciation. Once you invest in any business, two things could happen: your business will either be worth much more in a couple of years or much less.

Fortunately, this is not what happens with a real estate investment. Real estate has shown a consistent growth pattern in value. Your property will be worth a lot more in ten years. It could even double or triple in value, depending on where it is located.

Inflation. Most investors wonder how they can deal with inflation. Real estate investing acts as a hedge against the effects of inflation. As inflation engulfs the economy, rental property tends to go up in value. Consequently, rental income increases.

As you can see, real estate investing may not be hit as hard as other forms of investment. Real estate investing allows you to make your decisions.

Some investments are demanding. Even after investing a significant amount of money in them, you still need to use most of your time monitoring them. Investing in real estate rewards you handsomely and frees your time.

Real estate allows you to become your boss. You get to manage your own time. You also have a lot of time at your disposal to engage in other activities. What's even better is that you have control over your property, and you decide what to do with it at any given time.

Moreover, you get to decide on which kind of tenants should occupy your property and which property management firms you should work with.

Investment portfolio diversification. Diversifying your investment portfolio is imperative, and it is best to do it through a solid and reliable investment. Investing in real estate can deliver the kind of diversification you have been looking forward to. It will offer you protection against unexpected eventualities such as inflation.

Regardless of the prevailing financial market conditions, real estate can always be monetized. This can be done by renting out a property or selling it. Finally, it gives you as the owner the coveted sense of financial stability.

It is an alternative means of saving. As you age, your responsibilities tend to increase, and so does your financial needs. Your children or grandchildren are probably approaching college, and you need money to fund their education. Retirement is also knocking on the door, and you ought to be financially prepared.

Investing in real estate is an alternative means of saving. It solidifies your financial stability and gives the much-needed financial freedom. As your children approach college, you can support their education without feeling the financial strain.

Ongoing income. A stable investment needs to bring in more than just a fixed income. The income should grow. Choosing real estate investing is a smart way to generate an ongoing and growing income. For example, if you purchase a rental property, your rental income is likely to go up after a couple of years. This happens consistently and thus improving your financial state.

Real estate can be leveraged. Real estate can be leveraged. For this reason, it is an incredible asset investment vehicle that you can finance easily. With real estate, you can borrow up to 90% to acquire a property. Moreover, you access the necessary funding at a reasonable interest. This is popularly known as positive leverage, and it is tremendously difficult to find with other investments.

Real estate investing extends flexibility. A lot of investments will barely give you breathing space. You will have to put in long hours to make your money. You might not have enough time and money to invest elsewhere.

Once you begin investing in real estate, you can do it full time. You can plow back your profits in the investment and turn it into a full-time job. Your salary is also not restricted, and you have the chance to grow it by expanding your investment.

Constant demand. People are always looking for property to rent or buy. If you make a shrewd decision regarding property choice, then your property will be in constant demand. This is a desirable investment trait as it guarantees income.

A high rate of returns. One of the characteristics of investing in real estate is the high rate of returns. When you purchase a property in a developing area, there is a chance that it could double its worth in a few years. Rental income can also skyrocket within a few years. Other investment opportunities are unlikely to offer you such high returns.

If you are targeting the rate of returns in real estate, choose your property wisely. Pay more attention to the location of the property as well as the rate of development within the area.

What you might not know is that rental properties can give you returns of up to 20%. You probably can't get such returns at your local bank.

Real estate is always worth something. Investments sometimes go haywire. People lose all their investment. But no matter what happens, real estate will always be worth something. Your property will never fall to zero. It may not be immune from losses, but you can never lose it all. When the value drops significantly, you can still sell your property.

Real estate offers a variety of choices. Some investment opportunities tend to be rigid. You only have a few choices to work with. There is no chance to diversify your collective investment in a particular field. Fortunately, real estate offers a variety of investment choices. You can diversify within real estate by purchasing different types of properties in various locations. You could invest in multi-family homes, condos, commercial buildings, or land. You can then tell which type of property pays better.

Providing home for others. This may not be a monetary benefit, but it counts. As an investor, it feels good to know that you are providing safe, secure, and comfortable homes to numerous families. Such a responsibility comes with a sense of accomplishment.

Real estate investment is not complex. Most investments come with a high level of complexity. When you factor in taxations and fluctuations of the prices in the market, it can feel like a gamble. Luckily, real estate is a brick and mortar investment that you can easily understand.

You know exactly what is expected of you and how to make your money. The tax system in real estate investing is easy to understand. Managing the investment is not as demanding as managing the shares and stocks.

The process of entering into real estate is friendly. Like with any other investments, you will need to learn a few things, but you do not need to be an expert to flourish in real estate.

There might be some skepticism surrounding real estate investment, but most of it is based on unfounded claims. Real estate indisputably offers one of the most lucrative investment opportunities. Real estate investing is a great addition to your investment portfolio that can outlast most of your investments.

If you are looking to make a secure, reliable, and stable passive income, then look no further. The demand for property is insatiable. Choose your properties right, and you will never struggle to find a client. Properties have appreciated steadily over the last 30 years. The ultimate truth is that you can hardly go wrong with real estate investing.

Chapter 2: How to Build Passive Income Through Real Estate

Some people are looking for other opportunities to improve their earnings. While others want to diversify when they realize their job is not safe (people being retrenched occasionally) and rearing retirement age. With these and other reasons in mind, people are looking into areas that can generate passive income. It is a way to enable financial freedom for people.

Someone who earns a passive income can maintain the lifestyle he/she was accustomed to during his/her working days or more. The benefit of passive income is that its earnings one can get without much fuss or little time spent on site.

Below are some of the best ways one can build a passive income through real estate and be successful:

Property Upgrading. Property improvement involves buying a house/property, carrying out some renovations, and upgrade before selling it for profit. For one to be successful in this field, there are a few tips to remember, such as:

- Not doing too much upgrade on the property - do not overdo the update in a property. Add simple repairs and renovations that bring color to the home but not too much flair. Upgrade the home, depending on the neighborhood's model. Not doing custom work and adding expensive pieces of equipment within the house, such as adding marble.

- Decide on the best neighborhood to invest in as value varies - areas with good security and can quickly assemble to social amenities are items people prefer. The worth of such areas will always appreciate, and it is in these neighborhoods you would want to invest in.
- Working with the best contractors in the business - some contractors can do a shoddy job, and this comes at your cost. You need to hire contractors that have a good reputation for their projects and are highly recommended in the industry.
- Investing in property wisely - the main aim of buying the property and upgrading is to make a profit out of the sale. For this to happen, you need to be cautious with the price of the house you are buying. The upgrade expense should also be within the budget to be able to sell the house at a price that is not considered overpriced.

Out-of-State Investing. Investing in out-of-state properties can be profitable when one knows occasional setbacks in the real estate sector. There are numerous encounters one can experience when he/she is just getting started in out-of-state investment. Below are some of the techniques one can employ to cope with the challenges experienced:

- Using technology advancement to your advantage - technology is continuously improving, and out-of-state investor needs to take view it as a positive change. Technology can sometimes be sophisticated for some, but one only needs to know to grasp some of it.
- Building a great team- in the event of wanting to invest, you need to have a good team on the ground to help with the transition, such as the right contractor.
- Carrying out your research- before investing in a project, you need to do some research to know the value range, security, and government policies required in that area.

Turnkey Rental Properties. This is also a great way of generating passive income in real estate. Turnkey rental properties mean an investor buying property that has already been upgraded by a contractor or newly built wealth. The investor then rents out the property.

Airbnb. Listing in the Airbnb is a good model of generating income while meeting new faces all the time. Airbnb involves renting out a room or house to people through an online connection. The business has its ups and downs, and for someone who wants to make it in the sector, below are some of the ways to go about it:

- Excellent customer care and management qualities- the customer in his case is a tenant or potential tenant, and so one needs to respond promptly to inquiries.
- Highlighting the features of the area the home is located, such as amenities available and the features the property contains.
- Excellent customer relations and also creating a good rapport with the tenants.
- In the listing, the photos of the area and the house interior can also improve the chances of getting a tenant.

E-Commerce Store. Creating an online presence for your property increases the chances of getting clients. In modern society, people are searching for their dream homes online compared to going physically. Research has shown that the number of people who bought their homes that were initially discovered through online search has increased tremendously. With this in mind, an investor should have an online presence for his/her properties to boost prospective client sales.

Real Estate Investment Trusts. REITs are companies that usually operate in generating income through real estate. The firms act like mutual funds; hence an investor has a variety of options available to him/her for analysis before investing. The investor is paid in the form of dividends. In this case, the investor does not get involved too much like the other options above. The work is done for him. The risk in REIT is minimized as the investor has a variety of options, and the investment is not made in one commodity but spread around.

Rental Properties. Rental properties are the best method sought after by investors compared to the other modes of generating passive income. The returns for this method do not take much time, and that's why it is favored. The rental property offers security and some guarantee of earning income monthly without much risk. There is a company owner's contract to manage the properties for them, and the investor sits back and waits for his/her guaranteed returns.

Eluding the Money Pits. When new in real estate business, the best advice experienced individuals always give is to avoid money pits. These are properties that will consume lots of money in terms of expenses in repairing the property and also the income generated. The property does not attract interest from prospecting clients and ends up making loses. For this not to happen, and individual needs to do lots of research on a property before deciding to buy it. The study involves checking the local market real estate growth index, government taxes levied, and also the terms of investment. It is a long-term or short-term investment. Another way of avoiding poor business practice is by seeking the advice of an experienced individual in the sector before investing in the property.

Coming Up with a Strategy Analysis in Passive Income Generation Model from Real Estate Investments. For a business to experience growth and success, a lot of planning and analysis needs to occur. A business plan is drawn before investing in real estate, buying a company shares, and government bonds. The business plan is put in place to guide you through the challenges and make sound decisions for the good of the business. Some of the issues to be considered in strategic analysis of a real estate involve the following:

- **Cash Flow:** The value of properties varies, and hence, expected cash flow would also change from properties. A neighborhood with social amenities such as schools, institutions, and hospitals is likely to generate good cash flow after calculating expenses covered. The risk associated with such an investment is low compared to the risk of investing in a property lacking such amenities.
- **Tenants:** A property owner usually prefers an excellent tenant to a bad one. The types of tenants sometimes vary in the kinds of neighborhoods you have invested in. If a property is in an affluent area, the tenants are likely to be disciplined and carry out their duties as agreed. This

means taking good care of the property if its rental in case of damage, carrying out the repairs, and paying rent on time. While areas that attract low-income people, the property owner is likely to experience challenges stemming from rent defaults, destruction of property, and little communication when there is a problem or moving out. The risk all depends on where an investor chooses to buy a property. Due to the destruction of property and rent defaults, one has a small budget to maintain the repairs needed.

- **Property Condition:** The property needs to be checked by an inspector before and after renovations to get the nod to place it under rental. The conditions of the house should be of a good standard, and all terms adhered to. It is the inspector or a professional who can advise on the necessary measures to be taken or the kinds of renovations required to a newly acquired property.

Choosing the Kind of Investment You Want. This is where you choose between long-term and short-term kind of real estate investment. This involves selecting properties that will generate income immediately, which are short-term. Long-term investment involves one looking at the property appreciating with time, and it can be acquired at a low rate, as the investor believes the value will increase over the years. The short-term investment is purchased at a high rate, as the income generated will not take much time to be produced back.

Financing Model. Most real estate investors leverage the equity they have gained with their home by getting a home equity line of credit loan. The amount an investor is permitted to borrow is usually limited by conditions of loan taken with the valuation of the house. Others take FHA-backed financing loans to start their preferred investment options. The amount is usually around $200,000.

Generating Leads. Lead generations are generally the hardest steps for someone starting a real estate business. Lead generation can be carried out by marketing through online presence, direct mail campaigns, door-to-door campaigns, posters, and advertisements. A start-up can spend too much money and time in this step. Some of the techniques used to generate leads fail, and the investor is left with losses to bear.

Estimation of Your Return on Investment. The best formula for having a good ROI is by implementing 'buy low, sell high" model of business. This can only work by having reasonable estimations prices and expenses to be covered. The costs can be of buying the house, repairs, and renovations covered.

Negotiating Good Deals That Are Welcomed by Shareholders. Someone who can get good deals on a home is a welcomed skill to have. The agreements need to be useful both to you and the homeowner. This does not mean you pay too cheap for the right home due to the current 'owner's misfortunes. Do not take advantage of people facing foreclosures.

The Keys to Manage and Achieve Success with Short-Term and Long-Term Investment

1. **Great Organization**. The organization is a critical requirement for the real estate business to experience growth and success. Excellent organizational skills will allow the company to be able to know which tasks to be completed and be assigned various personnel. An investor signs the contractor areas to repair and renovate and other housing professionals' duties.
2. **Having a Detailed Record System**. Records of everything the investor does should be kept on file for future analysis. A good record can enable one to know if the investment is making profits or losses. The financial capabilities can also be deduced from the system. It is from these records that strategies are formulated for the smooth running of the business.

3. **Analyzing and Strategizing on the Competition**. For one to be considered a success, he/she needs to know how to compete with the market and emerge top. Competitions breeds' adherence to succeed, and an investor should not be afraid of competition. Instead, he/she should embrace it. For this to happen, one needs to study and know about the competitor's strategies and ways of conducting business. From these assessments, can he deduce the best way to succeed?

4. **Understanding the Risks and Rewards Expected from the Business**. Taking risks is an essential way of growing the business. An investor who does not take risks is not likely to rise or earn high returns. However, one is not supposed to take any danger; it is supposed to be a calculated risk. The business should also consider the outcome of the chance to be made. If the losses far outweigh the profit, then it should not be taken. Getting more information about the project is the best way of knowing what's required and the risks involved.

5. **Creativity**. Creativity is an essential skill to have to be able to stand out from the rest of the competitors. Your projects should be ones that stand out from the rest. Clients are more likely to buy homes that are built or renovated in a particular way. Creativity sells. You can embrace new ideas and models to grow the business.

6. **High Level of Focus.** As the company is a startup, it is not likely to make many sells at a go, especially with low lead generation. Remember, "Rome was not built in a day" and focus on the hard work and creativity level. Your goals need to be on a short-term basis as you grow the real estate business.

7. **Prepare to Make Sacrifices**. The challenges of a new business can be tough to handle. An investor needs to be able to make sacrifices to make it succeed, such as putting in long working hours. The family life can be disrupted as well as your routine.

8. **Provide Great Customer Service**. The customer is always right. Put much attention on making your tenant comfortable and responding to their inquiries immediately. A satisfied tenant is likely to reward you with referrals and being a good tenant. For those running an Airbnb, excellent client service is expected to make the customer come back whenever he/she is around and not deserting you for a competitor.

9. **High Level of Consistency**. Maintaining a high level of consistency can significantly improve your business and also maintain already existing clients. The commodities your property is offering needs to continue for the tenants to be happy with the services. This also means maintaining a creativity level all across your properties. A reputation can be built from consistency.

An investor should follow the above steps for managing and building a successful real estate passive income generation to be successful. The techniques can also aid in the growth of the rental portfolio, which leads to an increase in the passive income generation. When one decides to have several rental income properties, the amount of income generated will be two ways. The normal one is the revenue stream created by rental income. So long as the amount collected in rents surpasses the amount paid form of loans, levies, indemnity, maintenance, repairs, and property management services, the investor is likely to gain much more in the way of monthly income stream. It is your decision to undertake a short-term or long-term investment. With passive income creating, one can have the freedom to retire happily to maintaining the lifestyle he/she chooses.

Chapter 3: Real Estate Networking and Its Importance

Almost every serious business establishment is run based on a good relationship with others and connections. Similarly, you cannot ignore the importance of networking in the real estate business. Establishing trusted contacts in your company would guarantee you better chances of success in any of your business deals. Unfortunately, many realtors ignore this aspect because, maybe, they have not had the opportunity to see the robust benefits it offers. Networking is regarded as the backbone of any business across the globe. In this article, we will discuss why it is essential to take networking seriously in your real estate business. Read on to find out!

Importance of Networking in Real Estate

1. **Enables access to better opportunities.** Having a good number of connections will positively impact your accessibility and exposure to better markets. By having your network set up, you will be able to get better businesses deal because you are getting in touch with the right people. It will be easy to develop connections with high-end investors who can land you great deals. Having the right network will save you time—you do not have to look for forums in search of suitable deals. Instead, people within your network can get it

done on your behalf because they understand the field better and know what is right for you. Additionally, networking is essential in real estate business because it plays a role in generating passive income.

2. **You will not need professional advice.** If you have been in the real estate business for quite some time, you must note that it is very costly to seek professional advice. Many real estate investors look for expert guidance when they have the funds to invest but no idea where they should spend it. This can be avoided if you set up a good network with other people in real estate. You will not have to pay anyone to advise you; it will all come out from people within your system. Wondering how you can make this happen? By attending real estate seminars and joining real estate's teams on social media. You can even go to real estate investment clubs. Introduce yourself to those clubs, and once people know who you are, they will more likely be willing to guide you get a better perspective of the market.

3. **Education.** Not only will your network help you grow your investment, but it also educates you on the most recent trends in the market. Networking has been proven to be the best and quickest way to access new information. Networking events are not only based on interacting with your fellow investors, but there is a guest speaker invited in

most cases. You will learn a lot of new information, from how you can effectively run a real estate team to how you can maximize profits in your deals. And for your information, these talks and seminars are free as long as you are part of the network.

4. **It helps you increase contacts.** As we said earlier, having contacts in real estate business is one way you can maximize your chances of success. People are either buying or selling a property in real estate investing. Having more exposure to these kinds of people increases your odds of being able to be part of the trading team. You will have improved access to better deals by having connections with sizeable real estate networks. A network has every kind of individual in it: realtors, real estate attorneys, contractors, court officials, property managers, and contractors, among others. These professionals will help you identify the right deals and close them.

A team of dependable service providers is always required at any stage of your investing journey, whether you are a contractor or a lender. Most of these individuals attend the networking events held monthly, and you have a higher chance of connecting with them on such platforms. You stand a good chance of getting referrals or leads for your next deal.

5. **A great opportunity to have mentors.** The biggest names in real estate investment mostly attend networking events to increase their connections and circles. In most cases, such individuals are very generous with advice and mentorship. When you get an opportunity to converse with them, introduce yourself, request their card or their LinkedIn profiles, and connect with them. These kinds of individuals are the best source of information because they are seasoned and well experienced. Therefore, surrounding yourself with the right individuals in real estate lets you gain more knowledge and create a network of helpful and experienced professionals.

Tips for Networking in Real Estate

Knowing how you can build an active network in real estate is critical for any realtor in search of success. Networking is essential for any business to leave alone real estate investing. It is surprising to notice a good number of realtors not making use of serene networking chances available for use.

Discussed below are proven networking ideas that can be very useful for any real estate career or business ventured at large.

Tip 1: Surrounding you with a great team. Surrounding yourself with trustworthy and competent people is essential for your real estate business. You are only as good as the people around you. Apart from the team of professionals you work with internally, you can depend on the connections you built with other realtors within your network. Building connections with complementary realtors you do not compete with directly is a crucial tip to network. Put it upon yourself to identify and establish relationships with individuals you can refer your clients to and the other way round. This will improve your career network by large margins.

For instance, when coming up with a new property, you can rely on architects and contractors. While there is not a perfect contractor, having one contractor you can trust is a way you can complete your projects. Additionally, developing a good connection with an experienced architect familiar with the local terrain is also essential. You need to know the relationship between the contractor and the architect can strengthen or ruin the entire project. If they cannot work together as planned, it is more likely to create construction delays and inevitably consume into your general investment income. In situations where your client is not familiar with the process of lending, you can direct them to a lender you trust who can guide them go through stressful but essential real estate decisions. Having a well-maintained banking relationship will significantly improve your potential for landing a successful business transaction.

Tip 2: Create a professional website and blog. In today's digital space, your business should be treated as a digital media establishment: make it as digital as you can. From a visual appeal point of view, every website and blog tell a story, but the story largely depends on the character and listing description. In a bid to keep your readers well informed, a competent website needs to have new and original content often. An individual's first view of a place or business is not formed while they are at the entrance but built on the interior details before it is opened.

For your website to be attractive and outstanding, make use of locally known images and do not rely on property or stock building photos. You are not just selling a property or a building in many ways; you are trading an entire demographic culture. Display what you are best at by showing high-resolution pictures of your local area, your landmarks, and well-known sites. Research shows that photography plays a vital role in the success of any real estate website.

This will help you be the expert and scholar you need to be in your industry. You should research on which real estate applications realtors are using and keep an eye on fresh developments, trends, as well as innovations so that you can stay relevant in the business. Identify the real estate blogs and hashtags being used commonly and incorporate them in your website. What most people do not know is that in today's world, you can land a lot of deals just through your website.

Users will Google information about a particular property, and they might find their way to your website. Ensure vital information like contacts and location being captured clearly on your website. Also, take note of search engine optimization or SEO. Ensure much of your content is ranked on page one of Google search results. You can so by writing a high-quality article and having them indexed through the Google Search Console platform.

Tip 3: Social media. Most people will agree that social media is a powerful tool to connect and reach out to your clients. It gives you an excellent opportunity to share what you know in your field and also a massive platform to market your business. To get the best out of social media, brand yourself correctly across all the pages. For consistency and reliability, have a common name across all social media platforms. Someone who connected with you on LinkedIn might want to do the same on Twitter: this will be difficult if you are using different names on each. These pages must be updated regularly. The most recommended rate is two updates per day. What you share on these platforms will also impact the response 'don't be too dull' and 'don't be too 'childish' at the same time. Post engaging content that will attract the attention of anyone, even those not in real estate.

On a platform like Twitter, ensure you are only following accounts that are related to what you do. Following irrelevant accounts will result in too much-unwanted traffic that would make you think you are growing, which is not the case. It is better to have 1,000 followers that are relevant to your business than have 10,000 of them who have no idea what you do. To increase your connections even further, you can do a sponsored post that will reach a higher number of people through accurate targeting.

Platforms like Facebook and LinkedIn have a particular target criterion that allows you to reach out to any individual, location, or professional. To maximize your potential, ensure you respond to all inquiries, direct messages, and emails on time. Have a good interaction with your users, share new information, and keep them guessing what you are going to share next. Make yourself very approachable and be an active user across many platforms. For your information, social media accounts for up to 35% of established real estate companies' sales. Companies like Trulia and Zillow have attributed over 50% of sales on social media campaigns. Therefore, social media is a great platform because you can increase your network.

Tip 4: Go to conferences and real estate events. Networking events in real estate are excellent platforms to engage with other realtors in your industry. You can use these conferences to gain more knowledge and new information that your colleagues are using. Sharing the information you have learned in real-time on social media will increase feedback and engagements. And don't just get networks within your local area, go beyond.

You are more likely to have a connection with realtors within your area; therefore, try to broaden your demographic network by creating relationships with professionals from different regions. The fresh links will give you new ideas and suggestions on what it takes to thrive in their areas. You will now know what you need to invest in a different geographical location other than yours. Do you want to strengthen and maintain your connections? You can always look up your past and existing relationships for a cup of coffee!

Tub Richardson, an established real estate investor, says that for you to avoid losing out on your existing connections in pursuit of new ones, you should always ensure constant communication with them. He advises you not to go for an entire week without reaching out to them even if it is not official business. You can talk about football and how your favorite teams are performing;

it should not be business all the time. Tub advises that for a relationship to remain firm, it should involve all the three aspects of life: economic, social, and political. Talking more of business will make your connection think you are only using them for business gains, and you do not care about what they are going through personally or what they are feeling.

Tip 5: Engaging the local community. Learning how you can work well with different people and get associated with various charity organizations is essential in networking. Establishing a robust and consistent presence within your community is very important for any real estate developer. You cannot ignore how critical participating actively in community affairs is. Not only will community involvement broaden your client reach but also improve knowledge of your neighborhood and the properties situated within it. Wondering how you can get involved in the community affairs? Below are some suggestions:

- **Sponsorship Programs**: Sponsor school events, basic festivals, or even championship teams. Becoming a community sponsor secures you a spot on business prints, flyers, t-shirts, and program handouts. It is a perfect platform to market your business and build image recognition. Deciding to sponsor in a local team that plays in the national league, for instance, will put your brand's name on the national map. Things will even get better when that team performs well or wins a championship. Companies like Zillah and Grayson have invested in their local football teams, and it has paid off pretty much. Many people know them just because they chose to support local groups. Trust me, when a strong supporter of that team wants to do business in real estate, he will approach the company that sponsors his favorite team.

- **Volunteer:** Spend a significant part of the time on local groups and institutions. When you prefer sticking within the real estate topic, you can volunteer at local Homes for Humanity initiative in the area or work with a local housing advocacy organization within your town. This is an excellent way to broaden your network and have a reputable effect on the community, as well. You can come with your charity organization that helps shelter the homeless by building houses for them. For instance, partner with local leadership to identify those in need and establish ways you can help them out.
- **Local Media**: Reach out to your local radio and television stations. The right way is appearing on a popular show and talk about what you do. You can also do radio and television adverts to reach out to the local audience. Newspapers are also good. Have your business featured in them and watch your network grow. People

will want to associate with what you are doing because it is beneficial not only to individuals but to the community as well. Creative and funny adverts are more likely to be more exceptive compared to direct adverts. Therefore, when doing one, make it very interesting and captivating, something that everyone will relate to.

Chapter 4: The Best Ways to Finance Your Real Estate Deals

Gaining your financial independence and going ahead funding your real estate deal is usually never easy, especially for first-time investors. Though achievable, deciding the right way to support your agreement sometimes may lead to making mistakes that drive you to lose. You should understand that having limited money does not imply that you cannot venture into real estate. You can always utilize other options to fund your deal, hence generate profits, pay off what you owe, and enjoy your benefits. There are several ways one can choose from and acquire the cash they need to fund any given project.

But, first, you have to become financially independent by learning how to handle yourself financially without seeking help from a different family, friends, and colleagues, as well as other investors. The problem usually arises when funding your first acquisition, as it is a business you have never practiced before. Some may lean to their parents for help, while others may choose to become financially independent and use their hard-earned money to acquire the property. However, having limited capital does not mean that you can't purchase or invest in real estate.

Financial Freedom Blueprint

Becoming financially independent is one of the everyday challenges faced by real estate investors, especially when they fail to realize their potential in the industry. This is most common for those who are working and retired individuals. When you retire or still in the working industry, financial freedom blueprint is one of the options, which will enable you to do whatever you want without worrying about money. Becoming financial independent is another essential aspect of real estate, especially when your parents or other relevant groups fail to support you financially when investing.

Financial independence, therefore, provides an investor with the opportunity to venture into real estate without considering other parties, which may result in utilizing more money in the process. However, you should know that achieving financial independence or freedom demand a strategic and personalized plan as well as the habit to stick to the program. In this case, you need to learn the steps to achieve financial independence and stand by yourself, especially when you want to invest.

Steps to Achieve Financial Independence

Step 1: Control your money. People frequently tend to spend more than what they earn and usually avoid talking about it since it is scary. As to control your money, you first need to understand your earnings and how you spend, including monthly bills and expenses. Begin by developing a budget and allocate your payment from the most vital spending to the least and less essential elements. This will enhance saving money, and the more you save, the better. Create budget categories that enable you to learn your pattern while getting rid of debts and loans quickly to ensure your savings are not altered in any way. In this case, you will have a clear picture of your finances, thus managing your capital, retirement plan, investments, and net worth.

Step 2: Get rid of unnecessary spending. After you have understood how you spend and use the money on some unnecessary essentials, now you have to start trimming and working to achieve financial independence. Learning your spending does not mean that you have achieved financial freedom but the simplifications of how to spend. The next step is to sacrifice and eliminate spending, which you can do without. This is done by trimming your budget, and over time, you will see your money starting to grow. You can hence cut down recurring expenses such as gym memberships, music services, and more to achieve financial independence. Though it may seem tricky, it is vital to develop your financial freedom.

Step 3: Improve returns and productivity. In some cases, trimming your budget may become a bit challenging hence skip to the next level, which includes increasing your earnings and generate extra money. This can be done by either increasing your productivity or asking for a raise while putting your reasons in place. In case you fail to find ways to increase your income, look for other means such as working in more than one job or looking for a well-paying source of income. It is said that those who change jobs frequently tend to earn more and have a good capital flow, therefore, having significant financial independence. Apart from your job, you can engage in part-time jobs such as babysitting, Uber driving, and Poshmark, which typically doubles your income at the end of the month.

Step 4: Multiply the rate of your savings. You can also engage in passive income where you make money from jobs that do not require spending more time doing. This is essential, especially for people who lack time to engage in part-time jobs apart from their primary earnings. You can do this by investing in investments that do not consume most of your income, such as stock markets, rental properties, index funds, and mutual funds, among others. However, do not engage in the high effort and risky investments as they may lead to loss of money, therefore, affecting your budget and pattern of saving. This, thus, enables you to multiply your savings rate each month, hence increasing your net worth annually.

Step 5: Select the correct tools. Achieving financial independence also consists of different tools that smoothen your strategies, especially in monitoring your progress. These tools are crucial in budgeting, regulating investments, increase savings, and providing challenges for improvements. The best tools should, therefore, comprise of beneficial aspects to make you do anything without worrying about money. Some of the commonly used tools include betterment guides, capital gain, and fundraise. These tools primarily focus on achieving the best through an increase in savings, cutting budgets, and promoting your annual earnings. As much, consider having a tool to help in the management of finances more so when you have difficulties doing it yourself.

Step 6: Engage in professional investments. This is another investment step, but you engage in much riskier and higher-earning investments if you are willing to diversify your income. You can have more than one investment plan and involve several advanced investment techniques. For example, if you have a retirement account, you can maximize or extend to other 401k and IRA areas, enabling you to earn more at lower fees. Besides, ensure that you have an understanding of where you are putting your money as not to incur losses in the process. In some cases, you may choose to diversify these investments into different sectors where you are knowledgeable at therefore building your financial independence over time. If you want to have a complete financial freedom blueprint, then you have to learn and live like how most people will not.

Effective Ways to Finance Your Real Estate Deal

Conventional Loans. One of the ways to fund your real estate deal is through the use of conventional loans, which are the type of mortgage. You can acquire a traditional loan by first providing down payment, and in turn, the bank will give you the remainder of the money with the lien of the property acting as security. Most banks allow borrows to have a down payment of 5%, but real estate investors pay more of up to 20% and not subject to Private Mortgage Insurance. This is one of the best choices for investors to create income from real estate and unsuitable for those who flip houses.

Some of the benefits of conventional loans are that they come at the lowest interest, quick to understand, less burdensomeness, commonly available, and you can qualify even with a credit score of as low as 720. When compared to other loans such as VA and FHA, conventional loans are more favorable to real estate investors. However, they also come with some detrimental situations, which include the limit of how many times you can borrow, the credit score should be higher than 640, requires an origination fee, and challenging to acquire when borrowing through Limited Liability Company or LLC.

Adjustable-Rate Mortgage. This is another type of mortgage loan, but as the name suggests, it fluctuates with the variation of market interest value of the property. Your interest rates are the primary target of this method and are adjusted throughout the term of the loan until when you clear the remaining amount. However, there are cases where your loan can be altered through the hybrid adjustable-rate mortgage. Hybrid adjustments are where your loans are kept fixed over a certain period of years and later transition into adjustable rates. This method of funding real estate may result in increased investment capital; therefore, it may result in a risk for losses.

However, adjustable-rate mortgage accompanies multiple benefits, which include reduced initial interests than when compared to fixed mortgages. Another advantage is that the interest rates may decrease over some years, and it is ideal for short-term loans as the rates usually increase over prolonged periods. The disadvantages, on the other hand, are difficult to understand and evaluate how they operate, the chances of an increase in rates according to history, and the challenge of predicting the prices. Though beneficial to short-term borrowers, real estate investors to fund their deals can consider this method and have their investment capital at hand.

Hard Money. Hard money is another form of funding your real estate deal and uses the property to secure the loan. This form is similar to private money lending, but instead of getting money from individual people such as family and friends, you use your hard assets to secure the loan. The money borrowed is usually short-term lending, and the borrower receives a cover of between 70%-80% of the purchase price. Therefore, the lenders ensure that the property is usually worth more than the loan but come at higher interest rates and other fees.

Some of the benefits of hard money include flexibility in loan structures, and borrowers can qualify easily as the loan is secured with the property and can be found easily. More so, hard money loans are quickly approved, as lenders understand the uniqueness of the borrowing, therefore, hasten the turnaround period. On the other hand, hard money also accompanies its disadvantages. One of them includes higher interest rates of up to 12% and therefore becomes more expensive and perceived risky. The repayment period is usually shorter, a year, or less. Besides, if you choose to rent the house, then you are required to refinance it, which is difficult and more expensive.

Federal Housing Authority (FDA) Loans. These are government-sponsored loans influencing people to purchase homes by providing borrowing options with a down payment of 3.5%. Unlike other real estate loans such as conventional, FHA guarantees the money to borrowers, therefore, taking significant financial risks on repayments. As such, borrowing is quite straightforward as the general public qualifies but specific parameters, while the lender is ensuring competitive interest rates. As the lender takes risks when lending, the loan usually accompanies strict measures to guarantee repayment in case a borrower defaults.

The benefits of FDA loans include reduced down payments with some demanding for closing charges and relaxed qualification standards with a credit score of between 550 and 600. The disadvantages of this method of funding real estate deals are that you are required to live in the house for at least one year and the limit of having one loan at one time. Besides, your property has to undergo an assessment to inspections to establish its market value, and the approval may take longer than the conventional loan. The version of the loan is usually the Mortgage Insurance Premium rather than the Private Mortgage Insurance, and therefore you have to pay the loan throughout its life. Besides, there exist stricter appraisal and inspection obligations, which make the loans nearly impossible to obtain.

Veteran Affairs (VA) Loans. This is a type of mortgage or real estate loan primarily for those who serve or have served in the military and the best form of funding your real estate deal. However, banks now offer this type of loan to different people linked to veterans, and qualifying for this type is of loan comes with significant advantages. When applying, the loan has no down payment to veterans, military spouses, and service members. Like FDA loans, you are also required to live in the property for at least a year and then buy as many houses as you want based on your entitlement amount.

As mentioned, one of the enormous benefits of VA loans is that it has no down payment though accompanies closing costs but comes with the lowest interest rates. The PMI is also not required, and the borrower can purchase different houses with the loan when they qualify. Similarly, the debt-to-income ratio is quite higher, making you develop a portfolio of real estate by only living in each for at least a year. The main disadvantage of these VA loans is that not everyone can access it, and for those who qualify tend to have complicated paperwork to obtain the loan. The borrower is required to live in the property for a year or more, and the funding fee of the VA is occasionally added into the loan.

Home Equity Line of Credit (HELOC). Home equity line of credit, commonly referred to as HELOC, is a type of real estate fund, which enables investors to break the ties of equity attached to their property. That is when you have a home, and there are loans tied to it, you can acquire HELOC to tap into the property, which has appreciated since you took your mortgage. For example, if you had a mortgage of $250,000 and already established a house and lived for ten years, the appreciation may double the amount to up to $500,000. However, the value of the property may affect the need to invest in another deal and enjoy the benefits of real estate. In this case, you will acquire HELOC from the remainder of the property value free from the initial mortgage to fund another deal.

This is another beneficial form of funding a new investment, especially when you have an existing mortgage loan for your new project. The benefits include the inexpensive terms of closing costs and rates as well as an excellent form of leverage to build your assets. The loan is also flexible, and you can pay it off anytime you want due to its flexibility and reduced closing charges. On the other hand, HELOC consists of adjustable rates limiting the ability to predict the exact amount to repay. More so, it accelerates the costs of retaining your home as you spend the equity mainly for your home.

203k loans. Like FDA loans, 203k demand a 3.5% down payment, but it is more for homeowners than investors. The investment enables you to include rehab costs into your mortgage loans, therefore, building your funding into a specific deal. As a borrower, you will receive rehab costs, which are essential for sealing deals in real estate. The rehab costs are readily available, and you can negotiate your desired amount of the amount needed. Besides, you can fund the whole deal with one lender and widen your project. Disadvantages of 203k loans include the requirement to live in the property as if it is your primary home, vetting of contracts before approval, and lacks paperwork at all stages of settlement.

Guidelines for Funding Your First Real Estate

- **Learn your value.** Since the introduction of real estate investment, the value of each property fluctuates depending on the market, but the rental income remains the same in the leasing agreement. In other words, the market can do whatever it wants as the numbers work. In this case, when thinking about acquiring a loan to fund your real estate deal, understand that asset-based lenders often lend you money depending on the cash flow of the property rather than your income.
- **Identify your market.** There are different places to look when venturing into real estate, but when putting your money in a specific property, ensure you have the right one. Big cities are prone to stiff competition than when compared to other markets. Therefore, startup investors need to put their money on secondary markets where there are stable and higher rental returns. These markets are ordinarily vulnerable to providing high returns with other benefits such as strong economies and reduce vacancy rates. There are, therefore, the right places to put money.

- **Seek excellent deals.** Having a good deal does not necessarily mean that you have to go for modern and expensive real estate, but it means putting your money on valuable properties. When you have limited funds and prefer real estate deals, then move around trying to find excellent deals to invest. In some cases, you can find brokers to help you find the best deals. Besides, friends and family with experience in the market can provide useful information regarding finding good deals. This is an essential aspect to practice as primarily prevents engaging in misleading and dangerous sales, which may see you go into loses or take more time to generate profits.

- **Determine your investment capital source.** Today, there are multiple areas to request and get your investment capitals, including both traditional and modern sources. Conventional financing is usually from bank mortgages where you can contact or visit the bank and acquire your wealth. Advanced funding includes different areas where you can shop for investment capital. Some of them include crowdfunding, private equity, hard money, and bridge loans, among others. There are other options, such as the B2R program, which can be good alternatives to acquire your investment capital.

- **Closing the deal.** Getting the deal done in real estate demands for an attorney who drafts a purchase agreement as well as playing as an intermediate in the trade. The process of closing the deal also requires an individual to check for property liens in the title to avoid investing in a property with lien claims. Though rare to find liens in real estate, it is critical to have someone to ensure that there exists none. Once the title is clear, then you are now a real estate investor; start marketing, get tenants, and build your profits.

Chapter 5: Evaluating, Managing, and Adding Value to Property

Real estate is a property that consists of land and anything built on it as well as the natural resources contained in it. Property investment has become one of the most common methods of investment in the modern world. Most investors consider it due to the high returns as well as the demand.

Evaluating Property

When investing in real estate, property evaluation is very significant as it is the process through which you estimate the worth of your property, either land or buildings. Evaluating your property can be quite a challenging task, which requires you to seek assistance from professional property valuers. The experts will perform all the appropriate valuations successfully and come up with the accurate worth of your property. Various reasons can make you evaluate your property. Some of the reasons are discussed below.

1. **When you want to get insurance for your house.** You may find yourself at crossroads when you realize that the property you acquired had previously been underinsured. In such a case, before getting into insurance policies, you will need to get professional

property valuers to come up with the accurate value of the property. As time goes by, you buy new equipment for your home, thus increasing its value. Evaluating your property will, therefore, be important before you get an insurance cover for your property.

2. **Home valuation during refinancing.** There are instances where you come across mortgage deals, and right after jumping into them, you realize that you made a mistake. You may get yourself paying interest rates that are quite higher than you expected. Therefore, when thinking of refinancing your property, providing a valuation of the property to the mortgage provider is required before jumping into the deal. An expert value can help you get the exact value of your house so that you can pay interests that are equivalent to the value.

3. **When selling your property.** This is one of the most common reasons why you may need an evaluation of your property. You should get a good valuer to come up with the correct value of the property at the particular moment you want to sell it. The initial valuations of the property may be considered not as useful as the current value.

Steps to Evaluate a Property Investment

One of the easiest tasks you can engage in as a potential investor is identifying the property you could buy. However, after choosing what you want to buy, consider asking yourself whether it is good enough for you to invest in it. You must gain the confidence to achieve the goals you want in life by taking the risk. After identifying the property, consider evaluating it to and when it proves to be a good investment carry on and take it. There are four steps you can consider in evaluating your property.

1. **What is the property worth?** The first and most important step is the calculation of the market value of the particular property. Most companies selling their property use the abbreviation BMV to show they are offering their property at below market values. However, there is no such thing, and broad research would do you a favor. Market value is the price agreed to by a potential seller and a potential buyer. Assess the market value of the property by checking on much similar properties, those that are nearby, and those that have been recently sold. When you come up with the price of those properties, you can either decrease or increase the value of the current property depending on its conditions.

When evaluating a property, you can as well hire some experts. The experts will follow some basic methodology that will help come up with the market value of the property. They will also help you gain some more updated information.

2. **What will the property rent for?** When investing in a property, it is important to consider factors such as if it will rent, and if it does, for how much. You must conduct broad research so that you can easily estimate how much you can rent your property.

3. **Does property work for you?** There are critical calculations that you should make to ensure the property you are going for is the right for you. One, you should consider its worth to avoid overpaying. Secondly is how easily you can sell or rent out the property at a favorable value. You should keep three major investment goals in mind. These include getting a substantial discount, meeting a particular ROI target, and having strong growth potential for capital.

4. **Are there any issues?** One of the most crucial things when evaluating property is checking whether there are any possible hidden issues. Consider checking on the structural condition of the property. You can hire surveyors who can check on the general conditions of the property. You should also consider checking potential legal issues on the property. Some of the potential legal issues may include issues with the tile making it hard to prove the legal ownership of the property or dispute over

boundaries on the property. Some of these issues never come up when you initially check on the property, but when you are about to make payments for it. Always seek to know everything to avoid problems in the future.

Managing Property

Once you have purchased the property of your choice, the task is now on managing it. Managing your property can be a very demanding task, but with the willingness and focus, you can do a great job. You are required to have diverse skills and knowledge to help you balance the responsibilities and tasks of managing your property. When you do it appropriately, the rewards you get in return can be so pleasing. To become a successful property manager, some tips should guide. They include:

1. **Knowing your properties inside and out.** Being knowledgeable about every aspect of the property you are managing is very crucial. It helps you to answer questions that may be asked by potential renters efficiently. You should try to research every unique aspect of the property to attract the attention of potential renters easily. Potential renters will be assured of the quality of the property because through the information you provide, they know you have been to the property. It also saves

you the time of having to look out for the features of the property anytime a renter asks about it.

Another important thing to consider knowing is the surroundings your property is in. It helps you to provide potential clients with details. These details include accessibility of nearby shopping centers, access to freeway, schools, and restaurants. This kind of information makes the renter decide on whether it is the best place they should consider living in. Avoid providing information on topics such as racial population, crime rates, and noise pollution.

The more knowledge you have about your properties, the higher the chances of clients renting it out.

2. **Be dependable and available.** To become successful in managing your property, check on your dependability and availability. Consider responding to e-mails and calls effectively. Always be available when a tenant or property owner wants to talk to you. It helps you to build strong trust and healthy relationships with the people you are working with. Always consider being available even outside working hours by providing your e-mail to potential clients. This kind of availability makes the

clients confidence in you and assures them that they can rely on you.

Organization and time management are essential things you should as well consider checking on. To meet the needs of your clients, schedule your meetings accordingly. Ensure that you are present in the meetings on time, and you can effectively discuss the meeting agendas. Being organized in your expressions helps to show how dependable you can be to your clients.

The other thing you should possess is effective people and communication skills. When managing your property, you will always deal with people from diverse cultures and races. One thing you should consider a priority is an incredible customer service experience. This can be achieved by developing good communication skills. Effectively communicate with people without being rude or using offensive words to them. Respect their culture and beliefs even when they are not similar to your own. Ensure your customers are satisfied with the services you give to them.

3. **Practice good marketing skills.** Managing your property does not mean you become a salesperson. You, however, need to use the best approaches to ignite some

interest in potential clients. You need to have some confidence that you will successfully rent your property to quality tenants. You can consider using the Internet for marketing. It is great resources that can help you reach a wider range of potential clients.

4. **Work with a great team.** Teamwork is one thing that can help you successfully manage your property. The people you work with can highly determine how fast you achieve your goals. Managing property has many responsibilities that you cannot take upon by yourself. You must hire some experienced employees to help you with the task of managing your property. You can act as the property manager, handling most delicate matters, and delegating other roles to some employees. For instance, you can have a deputy assistant manager who all existing contacts can contact and a leasing agent who will work on inquiries made on renting and scheduling property shows. You can as well hire personnel on accounting, maintenance, and insurance.

Having a great team also enhances the decisions you make. Together with your team, you can come up with quality decisions on how you carry out your daily tasks. The satisfaction of your clients should be your main goal. The decisions you make should focus on benefiting your clients as well as yourself.

Adding Value to Property

The main objective you have in mind when investing in property is increasing its value. There are various methods through which you increase the value of the property. The methods include both low cost and expensive techniques.

Low-Cost Techniques. There are several simple things that you can do as a property owner to add value to your property. The simple things you do helps to improve the appeal of your property, thus realizing it's full potential. They may not cost a lot of money, but they can bring about a significant difference in the appearance of your property.

- Clean - Maintaining cleanliness in your property adds a great value to it. Ensure that you have a good garbage collection system to enhance the cleanliness of the property. The surroundings of your property should as well be clean and free from litter.
- Paint - A fresh coat of paint can add significant value to your property. It helps in brightening up the property, making it more appealing to potential clients.
- Stage the property - Declutter your property and give every room a particular function. It can help give the renters or buyers some effective imagination, thus adding

more value to the property. Ensure you properly place furniture to add some elegance to the property.

Moderate to High Tips. These are some of the updates you can apply to your property and incur some significant costs. The cost you incur depends on the level of renovations you make to the property. The renovations made usually make your property significantly valuable. They include:

- Adding architectural detail - Architectural details help to give some character to a boring room. You can do this by adding some elegant features such as portraits, chairs, or crowns to it.
- Changing or adding some windows or doors - This is one of the most valuable additions you can apply in adding value to your property. It helps to reduce noise around the home, advance aesthetics, reduce cooling and heating bills, as well as increase the amount of natural light in the property. You can consider adding some French doors to increase elegance or some skylights for brightening up dark spaces around the property.
- Changing the flooring - Adding value to your property can be through adding hardwood, changing carpets, or customizing tiles. These techniques help in making the property look more appealing to the eyes of potential clients.

- Reduce noise around your property - Everyone seeking to rent or purchase a property want to be in a peaceful environment. To make your property appealing, consider insulating, using double-paned doors and windows, and installing some rugs and carpets to reduce the footsteps. You can as well consider having plants around your property for the absorption of extra noise.

When improving your property to add its value to be careful about the techniques you use. Avoid over-improving your property at all costs. Always consider using a reasonable amount of money to renovate or add value to it. The amount you spend should be easily returned through the interests you make from renting or selling the property. Before the renovation, you must conduct some wide research to determine the potential value of the property after the renovations.

How to Give Back To the Market

Giving back to the market should be incorporated into any business strategy that you consider to use. There are several ROI tricks you can consider using to benefit the market, as well. Giving back is important because it makes you an appealing employer, makes your business qualify for charitable donations, gets you free publicity, and marketing, as well as giving you a feeling of satisfaction.

Giving back to the market is a social responsibility that every person considering to invest should engage in. Various steps that one should consider taking when giving back to the market are as follows:

- Making a plan - Like any other part of business, you should make a plan on how you want to give back to the market. Spare some time and discuss with your team the best ways you can operate your business to make the world a better place to live in. You can, for instance, consider using an invoicing system that will benefit the environment. It can help minimize the amount of money you spend on paper-based invoicing. The extra amount saved can be donated to a charity.
- Encouraging your team to volunteer - You should talk to your employees on reasons they should volunteer or donate some of their earnings to charity. Give them the morale to volunteer, which will be a way of increasing the involvement of your business to the market.
- Buy from neighboring businesses - One of the best ways to give back to the market is by promoting other local ventures around you. Consider leaving some reviews on other business websites as well as link them to other more prominent companies.

- Share your skills and experiences - Owning a business means that you possess some unique skills and expertise that you can share with other people. You can come up with some training classes where you teach other business people some skills they may be lacking. You can also train potential entrepreneurs on the best strategies they can use.

Chapter 6: The Best Rental Investing Strategies

Investing in the rental sector is seemingly increasing, with a lot of investors doing everything needed to be part of the industry. Getting the right property for your investment may prove to be a tiresome job, but you need a better plan and resources to make it happen. It takes more effort and sacrifice than you can imagine. However, thinking of the profits that come with an established rental property can be highly encouraging. Many people have done it before, and you can, too, if you are determined, hardworking, and are ready for what it takes.

Rental investments are fun when they are bringing something on the table. Mostly, after a great struggle and sacrifice and after a whole hassle of getting the right rental property, you will easily enjoy the success it comes with.

Rental investments come with several benefits that can encourage you to make that investment. These include the following:

- **Freedom.** Who wouldn't love freedom from being controlled and work pressures every day? I guess there are none. Most people like to feel in charge of their life. That is what you will experience after your investment.

You can make your own decisions and work at your own pace without being followed or judged for making mistakes all the time. It is a sigh of relief as you get to choose the kind of property or tenants you need for your rentals and also decide on what to charge for each rental property. In most cases, once you become a rental property owner, you get the right to decide on how to spend or manage your profits. It's a good thing being free.

- **Attractive profits.** Rental investments will always guarantee you a lot of leverage. Once it has been established and has a permanent or a temporary tenant, you will more so clear all your debts in a short time and keep on enjoying your profits. It is a great investment plan that will feed you and take care of you after your retirement. That's how powerful it is!
- **Exploration.** In the rental sector, you get to meet different people and interact with them. Research is an essential factor as you learn more about other people and how well to live with them. As you will be a new landlord, you need to be ready to live with other people who see the thing from a different perspective. You will learn to listen and change what needs replacement. You can explore a variety of places with different environments, and that can help you relax and explore more. Once you become a rental property owner, you become a tourist. A place that meets your objective is an ideal one during your tours.

What to Expect in the Rental Investment

Thinking of investing in rentals property does not come on a silver plate, as there is a lot of work involved to make it more useful and convenient. It is supposed to benefit you, the authorities concerned, and the tenant. Once you play your parts like a homeowner or a landlord, you will find it smoother and more peaceful in following regulations related to the housing act in each state. These are:

1. **Tax Payment.** For each rental property you own, you should be prepared for paying taxes to different housing authorities. It will save you from several punishments such as hefty fines and so on. To be on the safe side, ensure you pay your taxes on time and to the right authority.
2. **Insurance Cover.** Insurance cover is a useful feature and requirement of any landlord because you will have your property insured in case of floods, fire, theft, or landlord liabilities. Insurance means deductions in your monthly rent collection. However, it is not that bad as you are sure of your safety in case of any accidents or destruction.
3. **Repairs and Maintenance Costs.** For any rental property, there will be accidents that lead to the

destruction of property or the house. Either in the home or outside the compound, the sewerage, water, and so on. All these things require a proper maintenance plan and repairs. For everything in your property to function well, you need to make it more attractive by making improvements. All these require money, and there is a significant deduction on your money during the tax year to repair the damage and keep it in good terms.

4. **Not an Easy Task.** Investing in the rental industry is not that easy. You need to be prepared and understand what the sector demands from you. Consider putting aside resources that will help improve your rental property as well as buying a quality one. You need to do a lot of research and make time sacrifices to make it happen. It is not as easy as 123, as it can take a toll on your life during the first year. Being determined, motivated, and hardworking can help you make a life out of the rental investment.

Strategies to Use in the Rental Investment Sector

Some strategies can be put forward to improve your rental investments in any country. It can boost your business and make your investment worthwhile. It takes a higher plan to come up with the best results, and so makes an effort. These strategies may not be 100% but have helped several rental property owners manage and keep their businesses at its best. The following are techniques you can use in your investment and make big out of it:

BRRR Strategy

Using this great strategy will help you acquire more rental properties while putting more income in your pocket at the same time. It does not matter the time you are in, whether the times are hard or the market is crumbling. You should continue investing in getting more and more properties, and that will save you in the future. For instance, this strategy had worked magic for many investors who looked beyond the significant recession period to make it worthwhile. When people were suffering due to a lack of jobs and money to pay their rent or taxes, it was a real downfall at that time. The rental industry was close to death, but with time, it improved, and those who had invested in several rental properties enjoyed the outcome.

This strategy, also known as the Buy, Rent, Refinance, and Rehab, requires you to make the right decisions to save your investments as well as use it to acquire at least some of the investment cash or equal or can also be more. You need to be prepared to get the best out of it. Buying is a fantastic plan that will prepare you for better days.

Let us first look at the components of this strategy. They all work together to give you the best rental investment experience.

Buying Property - Buying a rental property involves many features that help you make the right decision and get something out of it. A proper investment consists of a lot of great deals. Finding a convenient agreement will ensure your investment takes a significant turn in the market. Make sure that you are cautious not to get a deal that will negatively affect your placement or make it lose value.

Finding a great deal requires you make a lot out of it, for example, knock on doors, sending emails, or making calls. You need to prepare for using your mind. Do not limit your imagination on what property to buy and what it takes to get great deals.

- **Decide on the rental property.** You should be cautious about accepting any deal in the name of good deals. Not all sales are going to work in your favor. You should make sure the numbers add up and can be used to make profits or improve the value of your rental property. In turn, it requires you to properly analyze the deal before you can decide on going forward with it. You need to make the right decision as that can make your investment go down the drain, and that is not what you want.

- **Learn how to close the right deal.** You have to be sure about how and when you need to close the right deal. Not all sales are the right ones, and that should be your concern. Learning what the agreement entails and how it will affect your investment is one of the things you should look into before making the final decision. You should first be sure and in the right environment to make the deal. The rental agreements will consist of money, which is not always a safe move if the deal does not work out. In most cases, banks do not like involving themselves in deals that are risky as that leads to money loss or the property. This critical stage requires you to give it the most critical attention. However, you may need to close the deal fast and start getting income.

Renting Out the House/Units - You need to get the right tenants for your rental properties to make the best out of it. It does not matter whether they are for a long term or short term. Looking at their profiles first before letting them in your property can help you learn how best to treat them to make them last longer. You need to learn the skills on how to retain your tenants, and I bet that would greatly help you get the best out of your investment. You should also experience any damages in the process, but be ready to mend and maintain them.

Refinancing - To make your investment more worthwhile, you should finance it from time to time. You need to make it a hobby adding something to your rental property to make it the best, more improved, and so on. It is crucial to have enough resources to improve your investment strategy. You can consider getting a bank loan or other commercial loans, which can offer you up to 75% of your property for more establishments.

Rehab - Look for the little details in those properties that add value to your investment. It should not be something that drops the real value of your property at all times. If it does not reach the required returns, you can consider improving it to make the best out of it.

Fix and Flip

It is a great strategy that can improve your rental investment in due time. It involves you buying properties that are distressed and later reconstructing and refurbishing them and selling them at a profit. It is not a very easy strategy, but it is what you need at the moment. If you believe you have the knowledge in the rental sector or the local markets, this technique is what you need.

This strategy will ensure you get the best out of your investment without having to go through a lot of the issues some investors in the rental industry go through to make it. However, you need to have a contracting knowledge that will help you get the real value of the property you have repaired. The repairs always take longer, require resources to look better, and need your effort. The right amount is bound to happen. You have to work with the numbers to be sure you are in the correct position in the rentals property.

Long-Term and Short-Term Rentals

Investment in rental property should guarantee you better returns. You can determine that by considering the long-term or short-term rental procedure. In the long run, you allow your tenants to live on your property for a longer time, probably several months or years. It is a perfect way of ensuring your income does not get cut short on the road. On the other hand, the short-term rental strategy involves you investing in rental plans that can use within a short period, such as hotels, restaurants, and other accommodation sites. These areas provide accommodation to their customers and charge them for the hours they spent in the room, days, or even months. It is an easy way of collecting income but may be affected negatively by repairing it all the time for the next customer. It requires massive maintenance and repairs, which can cost you more.

For the long-term rental strategy, tenants need to sign leases, making repairs on damages, finding, and screening the tenants before allowing them in.

Commercial Real Estate Strategy

It is not that easy to start and be completely established, but you can open your mind to other ideas. The commercial rental strategy is one of a kind that does not limit you to the private part only. You can show your potential in the retail side, for instance, offices, warehouses, business places, and so on. Owning a building does not mean you only need tenants to occupy and live in it. As long as you will get the returns you need, then any person, whether in business or work, can fill the rooms.

If you need to make more money, this is the best technique to use. Do not limit yourself from exploring more creative ways of using your rental property. You can try out something new, and be amazed by the outcome. It is an easy way of getting connections in the business world. There have been cases that a landlord turned to a business owner. It is a better way of creating much of your investment. As you will be learning from others, you will more expand your income channels.

More so, it is easy to manage commercial rental properties, as you will work together with the tenants to keep the place clean and in good shape with fewer repairs. You will also not have rough time-solving issues in the night. Most businesses operate during the day, unlike the rental houses, which need your attention during the day and night. This strategy can, however, work effectively in towns or developing areas. It also requires a lot of funds to start and to maintain.

Marketing Your Rental Property

Marketing is a great strategy to boost your investment. The more people know your property, the more you will get tenants or prospective buyers. You need to have techniques that are clear and have a better fitting for your property to make it more attractive and add value to it

Rental investing strategies are effective for startups or continuing investment plans. When used effectively, they will guarantee you hefty profits to help you grow more.

Chapter 7: Detailed Information About Real Estate Investing

Real estate is the physical property and improvement, such as houses, buildings, roads, structures, utility systems, and landscapes. Rights of the property give the owner the right to own properties and land. The real estate business is described as the profession that involves buying renting as well as selling land.

There are many ways of investing in real estate, which include buying rental properties, real estate investment trusts, and obtaining multi-family housing. REITs (Real Estate Investment Trusts) offer an opportunity of financing real estate projects and have are tradable interest like the stock market in a pool of real estate assets.

REITs operate in an income-producing real estate like warehouses, hotels, office buildings, hospitals, timberlands, and apartments. Most REITs operate and focus on one type of properties, such as shopping malls, office buildings, and apartments. Investing in real estate is different from investing in stocks in many ways; real estate investment is considered to be a long-term investment while investing in stock is short-term investments, and the transaction is very high in real estate investments.

Rental property is described as a property where the owner receives monthly money from tenants who occupy the house. The property may be residential or commercial. If the real estate investors are using a mortgage to construct the property, they should understand the mortgage market rate, which means if the investor gets a suitable lease, he will keep the cost of construction low, reducing the uncertainty of the future cash flow of the property. It is always right to weigh the cost of construction, make a form on LendingTree, and let the leaders compete to offer you a loan. At this point, you will have a chance to bargain and take the best deal on the table.

Types of Real Estate

- **Land** – This is part of the earth's surface that is not covered by water. The property is better ground, primarily when used for the construction of buddings. The subsection of land includes new land, land to re-use, prime development land, and site assembly.
- **Residential Real Estate** – Residential real estate is used purposely for the housing of human beings and an area that is set aside for construction or development of building for people to live on. The residential places cannot be used to construct commercial or industrial properties. They have been built for sale and commonly for single-family homes,

such as vocational homes, condominiums, duplexes, triple dickers, and high-value homes.

- **Industrial Real Estate** – This type of estates is constructed to generate income, including warehouses, manufacturing buildings, and properties. The property can be used for the distribution of goods, production, storage, and research, which is essential because construction and zoning run differently.
- **Commercial Real Estate** – This property is leased purposely for business or to offer the workplace to conduct business for tenants. Medical buildings or hospitals, education buildings, shopping malls, gas stations, retailers, office spaces, hotels, restaurants, and apartments are in this category as they are used to produce income as rent. Commercial real estate has four sections, which includes:

    o **Office Industrial:** Office space has classes: A, B, and C. Class A includes all the buildings located in the best part of the town, quality of construction, age of the building, and aesthetics. Class B is older than A and is not usually competitive compared to Class A, and most investors targets such buildings to restore. Class C building is ancient, like over 20 years, and is located in unattractive places and needs to maintain back the structure.

- **Retail Shops/Stores:** Retail shops are places of business usually owned by a retailer where the merchandise sold to the customers from the industries.
- **Multi-Family:** These are structures designed to house several families in different housing units. The structure may contain townhomes, duplexes, and quadruples.
- **Special Purpose:** This facility may be owned by commercial real estate investors but do not fall into any of the sectors mentioned above, such as churches, amusement or recreational parks, churches, and self-storage facilities.

An Outline of the Real Estate Business Industry

Real estate involves different types of job careers that individuals can occupy themselves in which includes the following:

1. **Sales and Marketing:** Sales and marketing offer jobs to many individuals as they all start at this point. Most firms deal with the marketing of the real estate business. Most of these firms work closely with developers to market the sales of the building units or apartments. This section is in charge of selling the company's properties. They also into the cost of sales of the completed inventory

units, and the firm is more focused on sales of the newly created properties.

2. **Real Estate Development:** It is a business process that involves activities that range from renovation, release of standing building, development of land, purchase of property, and constructing a building. People consider development as the most profitable type of real estate business. Development of an area usually add value to the land hence more profitability. Developers usually come up with properties that fill the gap in the market to create a new inventory.

3. **Brokerage Real Estate:** A real estate broker is a person who exemplifies buyers and sellers of real estate properties and works independently, while the agent usually works under a licensed broker to represent clients. Brokerage in real estate serves real estate agents who help in the process of facilitation of transactions between the seller and a buyer. They provide both parties with an excellent platform for selling and buying the land or property.

4. **Property Management:** These are firms that help the real estate owners in renting the building units. The major roles of the property management in real estate are collection of rent, managing tenants, fixing the deficiencies, and conducting necessary repair to the units.

Most property management firm charges the owner 10% of the total rental earned.

5. **Lending in Real Estate:** Most developers rely on leverage as a source of income for their investment; hence, real estate lenders play a significant role in the real estate sector. Examples of real estate lender are banks, credit unions (i.e. Sacco), government institutions, and private lenders. They give some amount of money to the developers at a particular interest and terms of repaying the loan.

6. **Professional in Real Estate Services:** A number of these professionals play a significant role in real estate in enhancing the operations of the industry. Examples of the typical professionals in the real estate are accountants, lawyers, interior designers, general contractors, construction workers, tradespeople, and stagers. Each of these certified professionals plays a vital role in the real estate business to run efficiently.

Why People Enter into Real Estate Business

Most people choose real estate as a career because of their growth rate. Denny G., a real estate broker, said, "Real estate provides a path to financial independence, a flexible schedule, and the personal contentment of helping families and their home. Few careers can do that." Since 2014, real estate has grown to up to 3%, and more people are choosing the real estate as a profession because of the following advantages:

- A real estate career is a quick process compared to the other occupations. The real estate profession is not time-consuming compared to becoming a doctor. It does not mean that it is a quick way of making money, but there are opportunities that one can utilize to grow, and people do it as it easier for them to get in.
- You are an expert. You will spend a little time learning how to be an agent of real estate and then nurturing your marketing skills. After the time, you will find out that the knowledge adds value to you, and clients always look for people who will advise them on the trend and market of real estate. And, at this time, you will take pride in your knowledge.
- Real estate gives people motivation for working hard. People who work in real estate and want to make a good living have to work hard and can be very rewarding, and it allows you to work as hard as you would want to compare to working for someone else, as you would not get the same gratification.
- Real estate is always changing. If you want a career that will not bore you, real estate is the one. If you are going to change a new trend in the market and adapting to different demands, real estate offers that versatility to

those environments that one craves for. While in the field, you will get a chance to meet different personalities of people and can be exciting.

- Real estate can be beneficial to people on their career milestones. The real estate agents get the satisfaction of knowing that they helped someone through significant time in their life. For example, a newly wedded couple buying their first house or a family buying their vacation houses. The agent gets the gratification of knowing that they are part of the people milestone and feel that they are part of the community. Agents love it as they are finding someone's dream house.

- The agent has the potential of changing what they earn. The agents are not limited to what they can make per hour of the month. They have a chance of improving their payslips since their career is their business. You sleep, you earn nothing; you work smart and hard, you change your payslip. Agents who are willing to work hard and put their clients first have a successful career in real estate agent business.

- You get a chance to be your boss. Real estate agents work as independent contractors, and they get to set their working hours and decide how you will manage your time and setting the priorities. You get to work from home office or anywhere you want. You set your goals and work on them and get a rewarding success. During the first years, you must put in long hours, but as soon as you get established, the clients will be looking for you as you will have repeat clients and referrals from past clients.

Appreciation in Real Estate

There are many ways to make properties appreciate in the market. The value of a property is clear when it is sold to a person and develops it according to the market needs. Refinancing a mortgage is a way that property appreciation is achieved in the real estate business. A land that has not been utilized in the outcast of the town lays significant opportunity, and enhancement of the properties by constructing an apartment can get real estate lots of profits. The construction company realizes the value of natural resources and materials in the land that increases the value of the land significantly. Property in real estate usually grows in time because the amount of real estate often dramatically can never be stagnant.

During the last decades, due to the increased urbanization of towns, the previous has become very expensive to purchase and construct. Also, real estate scarcity has had a hand in it, hence making them more valuable. The marketability tends to increase when the demand is high, and there is no property.

How to Earn Income in Real Estate

Income in real estate can be obtained directly or indirectly by investments of real estate. There are many ways to earn income in real estate; an example is a rent paid by the tenants who occupy the building units that were developed into commercial and residential houses. The companies usually pay some amount of money, termed as land rates, to cater for the land that has not been established. In case the owner of the property sells several shares in the property investment to different investors and make distribution of the rental income, these investors usually use the real estate security for their investments.

Terms Used in Real Estate Business

Business Home or Commercial Real Estate: These are structures or possession used for business purposes. The owners lease the building for tenants to use them to create a business that can be office stores, depending on the functionality of the tenants.

Lease: It is a legal document that outlines the terms of the party's agreement of leasing the property, and it belongs to someone else. Through the agreement, the tenant is given authority to use the property, and the owner is guaranteed some loyalties to the property. In case there is a failure to uphold the agreement, the two parties will face some consequences. The lease is a legal treaty that outlines the conditions in the property and outlines the responsibility of both parties.

Single Net Lease Agreement: This unique commercial real estate; the tenants agree to pay some property taxes in addition to the rent. This means that the fees that are directly linked to the property become the responsibility of the tenants. Such taxes can be land rates or licenses of the business.

Triple Net Lease: This kind of agreement means that the tenant who leases the properties takes full expenses responsibility of the property. The costs are the maintenance of the property, taxes, and insurance of the property. The tenant agrees to uphold this agreement, and on top of all that, they should pay rent. The rent, in this case, is relatively low as the tenants are taking care of the property.

More Benefits of Real Estate Business

When considering venturing in this kind of business, you should know the cost to incur and profit after paying the mortgage. In real estate, the benefits always outweigh the value of investments. Some of the advantages of the real estate benefits are:

- **Long-Term Financial Benefits Plus Security.** This is the best benefit as you are given the long-term security of your finances. With the consistency of income from the tenant rents, the reward of the profit is steady, and the value of the property always appreciates with time, thus giving you financial security.

- **Steady Income.** This is another best reason to venture in real estate, as there is a consistency in the cash flow earned from the rent paid by the tenant. Investing in real estate assures you that you have money to cater to your bills and some savings for emergencies. Also, with the savings, you are guaranteed to purchase another property hence increasing your cash flow.
- **Tax Benefits.** Owning a rental property gives you some benefits such exception of some taxes. In some countries, governments provide a break in paying land rates that caters to a potential in income loss.
- **Mortgage Payment Plan.** Once the tenants sign up an agreement with the owner, they start paying rent, and the money goes directly to the repayment of the mortgage. The monthly payment of the rent goes directly to the necessary reimbursement of the apartments and mortgage payments.
- **Appreciation of Real Estate.** The cost of investing in real estate is an investment planning for a short while as the capital assets increase in value over a short period; hence, your cost of construction is reimbursed quickly.

- **Inflation.** Most real estate benefits when there is inflation, higher inflation means the rental property income increases.

In conclusion, people who want to make it in real estate business have to work very hard and take extra steps to make their living better. You can work as hard as you want to and get the gratification for your work, not for someone else.

Chapter 8: Tips on Assembling an Incredible Real Estate Team

If you are a real estate entrepreneur, one of the best ways of conducting your business is to use a team of dedicated professionals. The real estate business has got various aspects that require the input of different professionals. In this regard, the multiple components of your business must be determined before deciding on whom to hire. This piece aims to explain the various advantages of using a real estate team, professionals needed in the group, and how to assemble the best team.

Pros of a Real Estate Team

In case you are a real estate agent, there are various benefits of working with a real estate team to conduct your business.

1. **Avoid overworking yourself.** To be successful in real estate, their vital areas that you must pay your attention to, including lead generation, sales and marketing, mortgage application, and others. Because you may not know all these key areas, you must hire professionals with the relevant skills and knowledge to assist you to operate the business. When you let the professionals work on various aspects of the company, you avoid overworking

yourself, and you will have enough time to attend to other matters of your life like family.

2. **Cost savings.** Variety of costs associated with the real estate business includes marketing expenses, brokerage costs, technology cost, and others. When you hire a team, you can share these costs. For instance, you may give each team member business cards to distribute to potential clients. In this regard, you have shared this marketing cost among your real estate team.

3. **Coaching and support.** In case you have just started your real estate business, you will benefit a lot from the training and support offered by some experienced members of your team. For instance, in case there is some repair that should be done on a house before it is sold, some experienced members of your team will assist you in finding the best contractor to use. Additionally, qualified team members will train you on the best cost-effective ways of conducting your business.

4. **Enough collaboration.** Although some real estate entrepreneurs prefer working alone, the best approach in operating your business is to use a team. The collaborative benefits of working with a group are immense. For example, you will learn about the best marketing strategy from your sales and marketing team.

5. **Helps in specialization and division of labor.** Working with a team will enable you to specialize

in an area where you are good at—surely, you can't be good at everything. Therefore, working with a real estate team enables you to concentrate at your area of specialization, which boosts your motivation and productivity.

Professionals Required in the Real Estate Team

To have a breakthrough in your real estate business, it requires various professionals. This section of the article lists and explains some of the critical professionals needed in the real estate business.

1. **Real Estate Administrative Assistant.** The role of the administrative assistant is essential, especially at the initial stages of your business. This professional can assist you in handling contracts from the start to their eventual closing, which will enable you to look for more deals. The real estate administrative assistant can also handle office-related duties, including preparing documents and welcoming clients.
2. **Buyer's Agent.** The buyer's agent role is crucial because it supports you in lead conversion, showing a client the houses available, handling any inquiries and needs of clients, price negotiation, and others. Because at this stage that you have an administrative assistant, you must

hire an experienced buyer's agent who will hit the road running and bring business.

3. **Inside Sales Agent.** The central role of an inside sales agent is to generate new leads. There are three kinds of inside sales agents: outbound, inbound, and outbound/inbound.

4. **Listing Agent.** The role of a listing agent is to prepare a home for selling. The listing agent works closely with a selling agent to come up with the best formulae of selling the property. The terms that they come up with are agreeable by both the seller and buyer of the property.

5. **General Contractor.** The general contractor is a vital team member of your real estate business. The professional will assist you in understanding the kind of repairs needed on a property before it is sold and may also determine the cost required to carry out these repairs.

6. **Mortgage Expert.** A mortgage expert will help you determine the best financing option that should be utilized when buying a home. For instance, if the buyer is a first-time homebuyer with a poor credit history, they can be advised to consider borrowing an FHA mortgage.

7. **Appraiser.** The appraiser is an expert who offers you information about the value of the property.

8. **Inspector.** The inspector assesses the property and determines its status. This role can offer you essential

suggestions on what should be done to make the property sound.

9. **Legal Officer.** The legal officer will assist in preparing the necessary documents, which are required to execute a real estate deal. In case you do not have enough resources, you should consider hiring a paralegal officer.

Tips for Putting Together the Best Real Estate Team

To succeed in your real estate, you must apply various strategies to ensure that you have the best team. You ought to consider the following to ensure that you have the best team:

1. **Put your house in order.** To have a great real estate team, you must have the best foundation of your business. At the foundational stage of your real estate business, you need to consider various things. For instance, you need to determine how much revenue you require from the company. The amount of income that you expect from your business will enable you to determine the number of employees that you require. At this stage, you also need to set up various systems that will assist you in your venture. These systems include vision, business plan, business promotion, IT support

system, the transaction system, and various financial and forecast reports.

2. **Determine whom to hire.** You must know who should be in your real estate team. The team should have critical roles like a sales agent, real estate assistant, and the listing agent. These roles have been extensively explained elsewhere in this post.

3. **Do your calculation well.** You need to calculate how much you will use for hiring the team, the amount of revenue that they will generate, and how much you will use to pay their salaries. In the end, you need to remain with a substantial amount of income because the business is yours.

4. **Aim at hiring a team, which will offer a tremendous service.** Your aim of engaging the group is to have them provide an excellent service to clients. The kind of team that you hire will determine whether you will expand your business or not. In this regard, hire a team that will offer a great service to clients. Excellent communication is key to succeeding in any venture. Ensure that the team responses to client inquiries fast and in a professional manner.

5. **Communication.** Communication is a crucial aspect of any business. Members of your team must be trained to be good communicators. In this connection, the team should avoid using real estate jargon when talking to

clients. The team should use simple language that clients quickly access. When communicating to clients, they should answer questions thoroughly and provide comprehensible responses.

6. **Hire right.** You must hire the right members of your team with the best skills, knowledge, and experience. This means that you should take your time to follow the correct hiring procedure, which will yield the best results. In case you rush, you may realize that you have hired people who may not be helpful to you.

7. **Team dynamics.** The team dynamics are an essential component that you should consider before hiring a team. In this regard, you must hire people with the right personality traits. The real estate requires professionals with specific characteristics, including strong-willed, lively, warm, and analytical. To help you succeed in choosing a great team, you need to apply various tools, including DISC, Myers-Briggs Type Indicator, and Larry Kendall Four Characteristics. DISC stands for Dominance, Influence, Steadfastness, and Conscientiousness. The Myers-Briggs Type Indicator (MBTI) also has personality characteristics that should be considered when hiring a real estate team including extraversion/introversion, sensing, thinking, and judging. Larry Kendall has recognized four kinds of real estate

agents that you need to have in your team: Category 1 to 4.

8. **Application of intuition.** Your intuition can help to determine whether a person is right for hire or not. From the initial phone contact to the office interview, your feelings about a candidate can help you determine whether they are the best for the role.

9. **Lead with why.** The best team should understand the vision, mission, and purpose of your business. The team members should understand the reason why they are in the organization and should align their energies toward this purpose. It would be best if you take the time to understand the personality traits of each member of your team. After this, apply emotional intelligence to align them to the objectives of your organization.

10. **Fire fast.** In case a member of your team is not productive and looks demoralized all the time, you must fire them from the team lest he/she spoils the whole team. You need to understand that negativity is infectious and can destroy an entire team, which is goal-oriented. Your team should always be determined to achieve the goals, and anybody who distracts them from this purpose should be dismissed.

11. **Assess your wants.** Before you figure out whom to hire in your team, you must take your time and evaluate your requirements. You need to determine whether you need

somebody to stay in office or a person to assist you in lead generation. When you assess your wants, you can decide on the kind of personnel that you need. For instance, at the initial stages of your real estate venture, you may require a real estate assistant to assist you with office work while you are out looking for a business.

12. **Determine your priorities.** Although you require a team that has all the necessary professionals in the real estate venture, you should set your priorities right and determine the kind of personnel that you need most. For instance, at the initial stages of your business, hiring legal or mortgage professionals is not necessary as the team can work smoothly without these roles. Your priority should be hiring people who will assist you generate leads, market your business, and help you in the office work.

13. **Experience.** When hiring, you need to consider the number of years the candidate has been in business. People with enough experience have the knowledge and skills of providing the best service. Furthermore, you will not spend much time to train such individuals.

14. **Understanding the basics of each role.** The key to creating a great real estate team is to understand what each skill role entails. You may not gauge the performance of a position if you do not know what it involves. For instance, in case you want to hire a listing

agent, you need to know what that person is expected to do in your business.

15. **Delegate.** Your aim of hiring the real estate team is to assist you to do the business. It would be best if you never stopped being actively involved in the management of your business. You intend to delegate but not abdicate. In case the team enables you to find much time, it is advisable to spend this time wisely so that you get more business.

16. **Trust and confirm.** The main aim of taking time to hire is to ensure that you bring trustworthy and hardworking members to the team. Although it is essential to trust that they are capable of moving the business forward and expanding it, you must do a follow up on any assignments that they are performing. It would be best if you verified whether they are meeting their targets by hitting the numbers that you have set. You also need to check how they are progressing at any moment.

17. **Have the right systems in place.** The real estate business has specific systems that can assist members in being more productive and performing their duties with ease. Before you think of hiring a great team, you should have these systems in place. After you have hired your side, you will train them on how to apply these systems. There are a variety of systems that your business may

require, including lead generation, listing, closing, and staffing system.

18. **Have significant subsystems.** The subsystems are those aspects of your business that makes it look great for potential clients. For instance, you need to have a professional platform and the best business cards.

19. **Learn the best practices of putting together a great team.** There are several resources that will assist you with the information and competencies that you require to put a great team together. For instance, you can visit the Internet and read books by authorities within your area. You can also consult professionals like real estate agents to offer you insights on how to build a great team.

20. **Team management strategies.** As a team leader, there are a variety of strategies that you can utilize to have highly engaged and motivated team members. You can motivate them by using persuasive skills and applying social and leadership skills.

21. **Have a plan.** Having a plan will assist you to benefit from your team. You need to figure out how each team member will help you to achieve your target of making a profit from your venture. Your business plan should capture your objectives, your purpose, the mission, and vision of your investment.

22. **Ensure that you recruit the right individuals.** You should have a committed and engaged team that is always ready to achieve or exceed the goals that you have set. The team should be prepared for continuous training and always committed to expand your business. You must ensure that the team members that you hire have the right talents that will enable them to perform their duties successfully.
23. **Right attitude.** The members of this great team must possess the right attitude needed to be successful in this business. This means that the team members must be motivated, aggressive, and always ready to learn new skills.
24. **Utilize the strengths of each team member.** Each member of your team has both strengths and weaknesses. You need to recognize their strengths and utilize them for the success of your venture.

To achieve your real estate mission, you need to work with a team, and building this team is not a walk in the park. However, if you follow the above helpful information, you will emerge successfully.

Chapter 9: Real Estate Exit Strategy

Having an efficient business model is one of the most important things real estate investors should work on. A good business model should encompass all the major elements involved in the real estate task. The significance of a real estate exit strategy should not be underestimated.

In any form of investment, a business exit strategy is used in describing the plans of either transferring ownership or selling a company. It is a way out of business. Many business owners usually come up with some exit strategies even before starting up their investments. They do this because the exit strategies give them a way out of the business as well as guide the decisions they make for their businesses. The mode of exit a business owner decided to use entirely depends on the size of their business.

Real estate exit strategy are the plans made by investors when they have any intention of removing themselves from deals involving real estates. Making decisions on implementing efficient real exit strategies helps in ensuring success. A practical approach maximizes the profits and minimizes risks to the real estate investor.

Several real estate investors lack the basic knowledge of strategies to exit real estate investments. This makes them incur huge losses, as they cannot effectively exit the investment. However, there are various exit strategies that provide a guide to real estate investors. The guide equips real estate investors with the knowledge to make sound decisions when choosing real estate exit strategies.

Importance of Real Estate Exit Strategies

Exit strategies are essential because they guide investors into making sound decisions all throughout their investment deal. They also dictate how well real estate investors can maximize their profits. Implementing agreements quickly is of great importance during the facilitation of transactions; however, coming up with effective exit strategies is essential before initiating the deal.

Evaluating potential exit strategies ensures that an investor has a sound plan for each property they are about to invest in. They have in mind how they expect to profit from each investment before meeting with potential sellers.

Being familiar with diverse exit strategies minimizes the risk of losses a business can go through. It also helps investors to save thir entire career. Considering exit strategies when getting into a deal also increases the chances of making huge profits.

In many cases, investors get into the real estate investment and later realize they have lost their passion. They feel that the business is a burden to them and in turn, not worth their time and efforts. By having effective exit strategies, one can quickly exit the market without having to incur losses.

Typically, failure to establish real estate exit strategies makes investor regret entering the real estate industry. This is because they end up suffering huge risks and wastage of time as well as effort. It is, therefore, crucial for all potential investors to work on exit strategies before venturing in real estate.

Choosing the Right Real Estate Strategy

Making a decision on suitable real estate exit strategies may not be as easy as it sounds. This is because of the various factors that one has to consider as they plan an exit strategy. The most crucial thing to put in mind when choosing an exit strategy is the profitability of the venture. An investor should clearly understand every plan and how it will help them in maximizing the profits on their investments.

There are no particular rules that differentiate every strategy for specific scenarios. A real estate investor is required to do extensive research on the strategy that best fits their business. Their familiarity with some particular factors determines the exit strategy that a real estate investor can choose. The following are some of the factors to be considered when selecting a real estate exit strategy:

1. **Short-term and long-term goals.** Prior to getting into a venture, one usually has some short and long term objectives. These are things people hope to achieve during and at the end of the investment period.
2. **The level of experience.** One should consider how much experience they have in the investment industry. Putting this into consideration helps one to check on the strategies that worked before and those that did not.
3. **Property value.** It also helps in coming up with a good exit strategy that is relevant to the value of the real estate.
4. **Condition of the property.** There are particular strategies that will fit specific real estates. The conditions of the property should be put into consideration to ensure the strategy chosen is applicable to the property.
5. **Market conditions.** Considering market conditions helps an investor in deciding what would be the right time to exit.

6. **Supply and demand.** It involves checking on whether the business is on low or high demand and supply. It also helps in choosing the right time to exit the real estate business.
7. **Potential profitability.** The main goal of starting an investment is to make profits. When choosing a real estate exit strategy, you need to consider the profits that can be gained from a strategy that one wants to choose.

Understanding these factors helps real estate investors to choose the best strategies that can fit their business. They help them to come up with exit strategies that can bring huge profits and minimize losses on the other hand.

Real Estate Exit Strategies

Exit strategies used for real estate goes hand in hand with the investor working on them. Real estate investors should choose a strategy based on their options to allow for desired results. The exit strategy a real estate investor chooses entirely depends on how much money they are willing to invest in the property as well as how experienced they are. Understanding different exit strategies increase the profitability of a business. The profits come as a result of the investor being able to traverse even the riskiest deals. There are different strategies that real estate investors can work on when initiating deals in the venture.

Below are some of the effective exit strategies that can help real estate investors.

1. **Wholesaling.** Wholesaling a deal views the real estate investor as the middleman between the end buyer and the seller. In this case, an investor finds and quickly sells a real estate for a significant profit margin. Investors can use two methods in wholesaling their real estate. One of the methods involves selling or assigning the purchase contract to a buyer. The second method involves actual closure on the property and reselling it to another potential real estate investor. There is no personal capital invested during wholesaling, but a wholesaling fee is charged on the buyer.
2. **Flipping.** The exit strategy is also referred to as rehabbing. It involves selling a target real estate at full market prices, thus making huge profits. Flipping involves buying property, making renovations, and later selling it at prices higher than the original cost. One of the best ways to engage in the flipping exit strategy is purchasing a property under the market value during high demand, choosing an efficient team of contractors, remaining on it is budget and timeline, and later selling it for the highest possible prices. Consulting a rehab checklist can help a real estate investor to come up with more information on the exit strategy.

3. **Buy and Hold Real Estate.** The concept of buying and hold real estate involves renting out a renovated property other than selling it. Renting out the property is for the purpose of receiving some monthly cash flow. In this case, a real estate investor purchases a property, do some necessary renovations, thus adding value to it. When the value is added through renovations, rental rates on the property tend to become higher. Buy and hold real estate is considered to be one of the best real estate exit strategies because one can get assets to build up equity on. Choosing this strategy also requires one to be ready for all the responsibilities that come with property management.

4. **Seller Financing.** Seller financing is one of the most creative real estate exit strategies. The strategy allows the owner of the property to sell it directly to an end-buyer. The owner is awarded some monthly payments from the buyer. It is an effective method because it makes arrangements between the seller and the end- buyer more flexible. Seller financing allows one to purchase more property without affecting the credit score of an individual and for easier negotiations on down payments. It is also the best way for sellers to gain some monthly income depending on the agreement with the buyer.

5. **Leasing Options.** The lease option is also referred to as rent-to-own. It is a real exit strategy whereby the owner

of the property agrees to rent it out to a tenant and to give them an option of purchasing the property later in life. An agreement is made between the owner and the tenant on the period they are going to rent out the property. After the agreed period, the tenant has an opportunity of purchasing the property. After the rental period is due, and the tenant agrees to purchase the property, their monthly rent payment is considered a contribution towards buying the property. These payments are directly made to the property seller.

6. **Prehabbing.** Prehabbing combines techniques from wholesaling and rehabbing. However, in this strategy, little work is done in bringing a particular property to a selling quality. The real estate investor works on repainting a property, adding some exterior and interior designs, and replacing tiles or the carpet. Rehabbers then purchase the property and continue fixing it.

7. **Traditional.** Traditional real estate exit strategies involve purchasing property and engaging real estate agents in selling it. The price of selling a property is often higher than the initial purchase price. Traditional real estate exit strategies are quite attractive due to simplicity. Very few processes are involved, unlike in other exit strategies. The profits made when using this strategy entirely depend on the purchase value and the selling price. To ensure success in traditional exit strategy, real

estate investors should be keen on the purchase price of their property. Investors should also consider possessing good negotiation skills, research on potential sellers, and best-performing markets.

Investing in real estate is a great opportunity to make significant profits, and a lifestyle one desires. However, there are risks that can affect the exit strategy one considers using, including a significant lack of demand, tenant problems due to lost rent, unexpected maintenances that minimize profits, and poor property management that diminishes the value of the property or hurts the possible flow of cash.

Chapter 10: The Four Secrets of the Successful Apartment Building Investor

Investing in real estate is one of the best ways to increase your wealth, especially when you move to the right lane with limited problems on the road. This is done through understanding techniques that may get you through the common obstacles and setbacks experienced by many first-time investors. In most cases, new investors that are beginners tend to only focus on the returns rather than finding ways to build their portfolio. However, the investment industry offers the best secrets to put in place and become a prominent and most successful property investor.

Real estate investing has been described as the purchase, rental, sale, management, and ownership of the property with the objective of making profits. When venturing into real estate business, then you may choose to engage in any of the ventures and make good returns. Understanding the secrets for a successful apartment building can play a significant role, especially for new investors. The first step is usually the most critical; as such, you need to have strategic and essential procedures to go about and establish a stable foundation when planning and choosing a desirable deal. Therefore, the secrets mostly dwell on going about sealing your first deal and generating your investment capital effectively.

Secret 1: How to Raise All of the Money You Need to Do Your First Deal

To make money, you have to spend money. This is also the case in real estate, as you have to create an investment capital at first before deciding which deal to go for. Real estate investors have different ways to raise money, and the same can be applied when you are a beginner and want to fund your first deal. There are various ways you can raise money, and you can use your own money that you accumulated over time or acquire a loan from banks, private investors, family, or friends. Initially, you may face difficulties when raising your capital, but after you have done so, going about your project becomes quite straightforward.

Self-Directed Accounts: This is one form of being independent when raising money for your first investment, mainly when you have been saving for quite a while. You can either use your savings or other sources such as retirement accounts, individual retirement accounts (IRA), or 401k to fund their real estate projects. This form is usually a long-term objective as accounts may demand for a longer time to accumulate significant amounts of more for your first investment. More so, there are those who raise their capital from different accounts under their name and acquire the needed costs for their first deal.

Private Lending: As a beginner, you may begin by seeking lending from private individuals such as friends and family members. As mentioned, having adequate investment capital is the foundation of reaching deals you try to find. Other than family members, you can also contact individual investors whom you are familiar with and provide you with a helping hand to invest your first deal. These are informal ways of raising money as it involves private individuals capable of lending you money without strict policies or restrictions. You can use the property as securities for the loan rather than have the money if you have an excellent relationship with them.

Institutional Loans: Another form of raising money for your first deal is through borrowing from financial institutions such as banks or other associated facilities. Banks are the most common sources of loans used by investors that come in different forms, such as FHA, conventional, and veteran loans. Both traditional and modern loans are suitable for your first deal but come in various types in terms of repayment instructions, interest rates, and closing fees. Some may become higher than others but with accompanying benefits than others. There are also private institutions that offer these loans and include hard money, wholesaling, and private placement memorandums.

Secret 2: How to Get Your Offer Accepted Without Experience or Proof of Funds

Before going about your deal, you should understand that there are others out there with almost similar projects administered to the same client. Similarly, you may have limited knowledge of how to deliver and get it approved without any instances of proofing your funds. This is, therefore, the secret for you and makes your first or subsequent offer to get an approval. One of the essential ways to make it accepted without any experience or proof of funds is through presenting it in person. That is, meet your client or the relevant party in person. This, with no doubt, develops the confidence to the other party that your proposal is preferably genuine with limited issues.

Another crucial technique is through accompanying your offer with the relevant addendums and documentation, which significantly provides a sense of genuine offer. Ensure you have an inspection contingency done while including any other relevant information and elements needed in the proposal. Other essential factors to put in place involve asking for seller concessions, buyer to have earnest money with the project and close the deal sooner to eliminate any other concerns that may arise. Even with limited experience in the market, having a strategic plan of getting your offer accepted without knowledge or proof of funds is also crucial as, in some cases, money may become a limiting factor in the deal.

Secret 3: How to Analyze Deals and Make Offers in 10 Minutes

As an investor, making and finalizing is one of the greatest achievements, which significantly promote your experience and profits in the sector. However, buying and selling real estate is time-consuming, as you have to go through different deals before determining which to choose. Besides, you may go through many transactions, and after submitting to one, it ends up being rejected. This way, you end up losing a lot of time without any accomplishment at the end. Then, you have to learn the secret of analyzing and finalize deals within no time. You can, therefore, examine the deal using both qualitative and quantitative methods.

Qualitative Method: This type of analysis comprises putting yourself in the shoes of your tenants and tries to figure out the advantages and disadvantages of the apartments. As an investor, you have to try and imagine how the real estate will look if you were a tenant, for instance, before agreeing to the deal. The use of qualitative tests using the 'I' and 'Me' enables you to ask questions, which are likely for your tenants to ask before they rent your apartments. Ensure that the results are positive and wanting while avoids investing in real estate with numerous queries from the tenants. That said, investors should, therefore, use a qualitative method of analysis, which gives them a complete view of how their real estate investment strategy is likely to be viewed by the tenants who are the target population for generating profits.

Quantitative Method: You can again analyze the property in terms of cash flow, which should be considerably higher and steady, therefore increasing your wealth over time. Focus on the appreciation and positive income, primarily when all the expenses are settled. The rent-to-value ratio is one factor in determining your cash flow, as well as the use of principal and interest (PI) payment to determine your loan payment and the income in a given period. The use of qualitative and quantitative tests is essential in ensuring that you quickly analyze a given deal within 10 minutes and deciding if you can make an offer. Some investors usually go for profits, but need to make an assessment quickly and move to another deal for a guarantee of getting tenants within a short time after completing the sale.

Secret 4: The First Way to Find the Best Deal
Many people are flocking the real estate business, and finding the best deal may become a challenge leading to putting your money to unfavorable investments. It, therefore, means that the more people in the sector, the harder it becomes to find the best deal to invest, similar to supply and demand markets. Besides, it has become challenging to adopt traditional methods of finding deals as these techniques have changed rapidly. As to see what

others cannot, then you have to use unique ways that others cannot do land you on the best deals. Then you have to be ready to do what it takes to be unique in the market and find great deals of the day.

Ways of Finding Best Deals

- **Shop around.** When you want to invest in a specific area or in certain types of houses, you have to begin driving around your desired space. This is a form where you visit homes that are vacant or transitioning negatively. When you start moving around, start by checking houses that are of your choice or the area you wish to develop your real estate. Shopping around is an idea as you are likely to find potential properties with all the features you desire. In some cases, those who drive around tend to note down the addresses of each home they like and go ahead to make an offer and complete the best deal in town.
- **Purchase bank-foreclosed properties.** Another form of finding the best deal is through going through properties that have been repossessed by banks from previous owners. There are investors who borrow loans from financial institutions to establish a real estate but end up failing to repay. Banks or other related lenders will thereto repossess the property and list it as houses

for sale if they acted like securities. The lender will ultimately remove all the tenants and sell the house to new potential homeowners. These real estates have been often considered to accompany good deals, therefore essential for you. As such, when looking for an excellent real estate deal, then these houses are usually the best. However, keep in mind that you have to undergo an entirely different method of buying these properties when compared to other purchases.

- **Be the first to propose an offer.** In real estate investing, it is not about the highest offer being accepted to trade a property but the first. In this case, when you want to have the best deal in town, begin by being quick when any of your desired property is on the market. Have a preapproval from the bank to allow you to jump on any property immediately; it is listed. You can as well hire an agent who will set up an alert for you to get notified of new houses in the market. Ensure you make the offer quickly or rather immediately on the same day to avoid losing it to other investors. Consequently, there are some properties that have been in the market for quite some time. These are also functional areas to find the best deals to put your money, as these owners tend to sell their real estate on discounts.

- **Contact homeowners directly.** Real estates have become competitive around the world, especially in the

United States, as many people can make offers on one property within a short time. Therefore, this becomes a challenge to land on the best deals as they also attract more buyers. One of the tactics to use to avoid scrambling is by approaching the homeowner directly and privately and proposes your offer. Other sellers may choose to sell their name through agents, and you can intervene and make an offer before they list in the market when shop around. In some cases, you can target absentee owners who may not be living in the property and make your offer. Contacting owners directly is one of the best ways to be the first to find the best deals in the market.

So, to conclude, you can never find the best deal when you only check at one or two sales and give in or wait for new ones; you have to be checking at different ones continually. The market is full of different apartments being sold, and the competition from other investors makes it tricky to land on some, which tends to be favorable. However, there is another option to find the best deal without considering those, which you desire to acquire. Even if you find one, which you think, is right for you, take time to go through the list checking out different deals. Despite being time-consuming, your efforts will pay off, as you will land on something perfect. Checking on various sales also opens up your mind on what to look for and what to avoid when analyzing deals with similarities. Narrow down on those you like most while eliminating those who do not please you. You will definitely land on the one, which offers the best deal suitable for your budget and needs.

Conclusion

Thank you for making it through to the end of *Real Estate Investing*. Let's hope it was informative and able to provide you with all of the tools you needed to achieve your goals in the real estate business. Despite the high number of people making the market quite competitive, you are therefore likely to prosper in the real estate world when using this guide.

The next step is to now venture into real estate, invest with your head held high, and discover the techniques used to become one of the most successful people in the industry. With the growing number of real estate investors, following these secrets to the fullest guarantees that you will stand out from the rest and find the best deals in the market.

Though obstacles and setbacks are prone to occur, using these tools will play a significant role in ensuring that no matter what comes your way, you can quickly correct it. Studies show that when you adhere to a given criterion well, you are likely to achieve the intended goal with limited difficulties. Therefore, the secrets will prepare you well and take you to the process of finding the best deal that suits your requirements. It does not matter how competitive and crowned the real estate world is, but what matters is how unique you are to achieve what you want